INTRODUCTION

"Who loves a garden, loves a greenhouse too."

—William Cowper

If you've picked up this book, it is because you have asked yourself an iteration of this question at some point:

If it all fell apart tomorrow, would I still be able to provide for myself and the people that I care about?

Maybe you answered no, realizing that you would like to take steps towards reclaiming your independence and personal security. Perhaps you answered yes and simply delight in reading new takes on the art of self-sufficiency. No matter where you fall on this spectrum, I have been in your shoes, and I want to assure you that you chose the right book. This book has something to offer to anyone who has the willingness to learn more about self-sufficiency. To that end, I want to teach you everything I have learned about greenhouse gardening. I hope to make you feel as secure as I do in my knowledge that I am armed with the information I need to feed myself and my loved ones.

We, in the developed world, have come to take a lot for granted. The uncomfortable truth remains that what we take for granted is not as permanent as we would like to believe. The illusion that food will always be readily available in restaurants and supermarkets is all but a placation for the harsh truth.

Furthermore, our minds are decaying as fast as our bodies. We cannot produce sufficient "happy" chemicals and hormones for our brain's health, whether through exercise or food. Gone are the days when humans were hunter-gatherers, foraging the forest for delicious ripe berries and fiber-laden tubers. Today, with our sedentary lifestyle, we are offered glucose-laden bananas and fiber-stripped rice as nourishment. We are so far removed from life, many of us not knowing how to nurture a plant so it can bear fruit. We have become overly dependent on mechanical processes, even for the little bits of nature that we can snag. Our supermarkets offer pre-cut flowers and already grown plants, giving us the illusion of the reality of nature. Now, we stay alive through industrialized farming, polluting our land, water, and food with chemicals that should never come into contact with our food or the human body. Somewhere between agricultural development and the present day, this is the world we created.

We are fighting a losing battle in a world where our fruit and vegetables now contain 40% fewer nutrients than they did in the 1940s (Long, 2009). Agricultural geneticists have favored modified breeds that produce more energy over species that give us nutrients. Should we want some exercise, so many of us are stuck in urban spaces, packed inside concrete landscapes with no greenery in sight that our options are minimal. We have become near drones, with highly limited options for eating good food and increasingly empty of nature. We are now so far removed from nature, the very thing that makes us human. As a result, our mental and physical health is deteriorating.

My name is J.D. Isaly, and I was trapped within this cycle for many years. I was spiritually, emotionally, and physically lost, continuously spiraling out of control no matter how hard I tried to center myself. As a recovering alcoholic and drug addict, I spent half of my life utterly destroying my body, mind, and soul with the most dangerous chemicals known to man. I lived my life completely devoid of nature, not knowing why I felt such a deep void in my soul.

I was given the gift of sobriety. Only then did I finally take my spiritual and physical health into consideration. Inwardly, I searched deeply and contemplated my life to find the areas that were poisoned. One of these areas was my food consumption and my relationship with nature. From then, I became obsessed with nutrition, food, and agriculture. I was hungry to learn everything about gardening because it was food that finally filled the void. Almost immediately, it improved my physical, mental, and spiritual well-being.

I discovered that self-grown ingredients make me physically healthier, and the therapeutic process enhanced my psychological and spiritual health. The repetition of tasks, the daily care and responsibilities of life so sacred, and the extra focus I needed to get through gardening became the therapy sessions I needed. Each time I saw a plant bloom, that was my enlightenment, as I discovered the unparalleled joy that spontaneous life births inside of me. In gardening, I finally found the center that had always eluded me. It rekindled in me what I believe to be an innate and sacred connection to nature, enhancing my spiritual well-being, making me feel good inside. Equivalently, it improved my physical health too. Working in the sun daily and being active with the physical labor of gardening boosted my physical health, which, in turn, released a lot of the happy hormones—endorphins. It was a win-win-win.

Due to my local climate making it impossible for me to garden through all seasons, I expanded my repertoire into greenhouse gardening. Why limit my favorite hobby to just a few months of the year? With greenhouse gardening, I figured that I could get more out of my garden too. The healing and happiness my greenhouse brought me only made me wish that I had done it sooner.

So, my latest passion was born, and I couldn't keep it to myself. It was here that my mission to help others take ownership of their sustenance to live happier, healthier, more independent lives was born. My spiritual connection to my garden was my lifeline, and I wanted to share my secret to vibrant, thriving life; when your plants thrive, you thrive. I have been studying approaches to gardening for years. Through self-taught endeavors, I became an expert at creating efficient and beautiful garden spaces under shelter and under the sky.

There was a time when I had buckets of passion and eagerness but zero knowledge or experience. As a novice, I spent years scouring every piece of material I could find, so eager was I to learn about gardening. The more I studied and spoke with those wiser than me, the more mistakes I made and cultivated a patchwork encyclopedia of greenhouse gardening. Now, I am an adept gardener eager to pass on my knowledge to you.

I hope this book will spur you to find your center and reclaim the goodness found on our precious Earth. I hope that you will begin to question the dominant narratives surrounding agriculture and horticulture and seek to discover what nature truly has to offer you. My sincere hope is that, after reading this book, you take away the tools you need to cultivate a sense of security and independence—in addition to some delicious produce.

This book is your beginning to a new life of serenity. It also covers some technical information for the greenhouse beginner if you have chosen to seek a new path. I answer common questions, such as why to use a greenhouse, when to use a greenhouse and how to use a greenhouse efficiently. So, if it really did fall apart tomorrow, you will be armed with the answers you need.

CHAPTER ONE

The Benefits of a Greenhouse

"We have built a greenhouse, a human greenhouse, where once there bloomed a sweet and wild garden."

—Bill McKibben

The garden is the epicenter of all of human life. Without it, there is no us. We feast on the minerals and vitamins that Mother Earth imbues in her produce. We survive because we can grow. History tells us that before the invention of modern medicine, agriculture was our medicine and science. Consider the historical culture of 'traditional medicine' present in many ancient societies; it was a lifeline for the sick. Herbalists and agriculturalists studied plants and their side effects as they sought answers for human ailments, passing these remedies from generation to generation.

In West Africa, the herbalists of the Yoruba culture became potent liquid medicine experts. From the bark and branches of trees and various grass and greens, they created teas that could relieve many ailments and restore health. The knowledge of these herbalists would lay the foundation of modern medicine today.

Nature gives us life, not just through our medicine but through our nutrition. The first pirates and shipmen of 'ye old times' would learn this the hard way when scurvy took over many-a-ship due to a severe lack of vitamin C. Our bodies – machines – require vitamins and nutrients to run well. When lacking one or more nutrients and our bodies will begin to suffer. The pregnant mother knows this too well, being warned sternly about the consequences of not taking her folic acid or her prenatal vitamins. Even in the life-making process, a human fetus is lifeless without mother nature's nutrients.

And then there is our state of mind. Many psychologists advise their patients to take long walks in nature. Our forage through nature has lifted many of us out of sadness, anxieties, loneliness, longing, and depression. The glimpse of a yellow flower, a ray of sunshine hitting a solitary mushroom, or the leaves trembling beneath the wind, creating a magical rustling sound, provides us with emotional sustenance. After all, very few of us could turn down a beautiful bowl of freshly-picked, dewy, fat strawberries—red and healthy and promising ecstasy.

Humans thrive in the bosom of Mother Nature.

WHAT IS A GREENHOUSE?

Did You Know?

If you picked up this book, you already have a faint idea of what a greenhouse is. It is a building designed specifically to grow produce within regulated climatic conditions. Constructed from transparent material, greenhouses trap heat from the sunlight within their walls and roof, keeping your plants warm even when the temperature outside is cold. The greenhouse, one of man's most significant technological inventions, enables you to control the environment within its walls.

Also known as a glasshouse, greenhouses range in size and capacity, from small and medium shed-sized to huge industrial-scale greenhouses that are the size of warehouses. Greenhouse environments are precisely controlled to ensure maximum growth yield and quality. As a soon-to-be green thumb, you will find that you can easily control the ventilation, light, heat, humidity, temperature, irrigation, fertilizer, and carbon monoxide in a greenhouse.

HISTORY OF THE GREENHOUSE

Did You Know?

The first-ever decorative gardens were cultivated around 15,000 BCE in Egypt. Before that, gardens were cultivated only for food and herbs.

The first recorded greenhouse can be traced back to 30 AD after physicians advised Emperor Tiberius of Rome to eat one cucumber daily. Roman scientists were tasked with developing a way to grow cucumbers year-round (Rimol Greenhouses, 2013). Gaius Plinius Secundus (Pliny the Elder), an agriculturist during Emperor Tiberius' reign, wrote about these Roman greenhouses. He described them as transportable plant beds placed on wheels, which allowed the plant beds to be transported into the sun on sunny days. On wintry days, the beds were covered with what is described as a sort of movable glass greenhouse. It was this greenhouse that was used to grow the cucumbers prescribed for

Emperor Tiberius. (Although initially thought to be cucumbers, these delicacies were actually snake melons or vegetable melons.)

In 1405, a farming paper compiled under the Joseon dynasty reign in Korea featured a chapter on cultivating winter vegetables. The chapter instructs the reader on cultivating these vegetables using *ondol*, the traditional Korean heating system built under the floor. This paper presents history's first report on artificially heated greenhouses. Furthermore, the paper describes how transparent windows and insulated walls will enable the plants to grow. These conditions permit sufficient heat, light and protection from harsh environments.

In his 1577 book, *The Gardener's Labyrinth*, English gardener Thomas Hill, described the use of greenhouses at that time. He talks about protecting young plants from cold, boisterous winds, frost and the hot sun. His description continued a tradition of celebrating the technicalities and the scientific knowledge of operating a greenhouse. *The Gardener's Labyrinth* would become one of many books that teach people this science for their betterment. In 1681, the first stove heated greenhouse in the UK was created at The Chelsea Physic Garden to grow medicinal plants.

By the 1700s, Andrew Faneuil, a prosperous Boston merchant, would build America's first greenhouse in 1737. In 1787, George Washington would build his greenhouse to grow tropical and semitropical plants. He grew lemons, oranges, pineapples, and sago palms. The Mount Vernon Memorial (2021), which preserves George Washington's home, describes the greenhouse as a delight cultivated for strolling guests. It was built facing the south side, with plenty of windows to capture the sun. Its ceiling was vaulted to promote air circulation, and it came with what is described as an "ingenious" heating system that transported heat from below the ground of the greenhouse.

In England, Queen Victoria built her greenhouse, The Palm House at Kew Gardens, in 1848—more than a century after greenhouses had grown in popularity, owing to technological advances in producing glass, making it more widely available and cheaper. The English' desire to feel closer to nature would quickly make greenhouses rise in popularity during the 18th century, although it was still only the rich who could afford them. In the United States, greenhouses also became more popular in the 1800s after glass became more affordable.

Greenhouses became affordable for the everyday man by the 1960s. The availability of wider sheets of polyethylene film made it easier to produce greenhouses. By the next decade, polyethylene film durability increased after UV-inhibitors were created, an innovation that advanced the quality and improved the film's usable life, from under two years to more than four years in many cases.

The future of greenhouses has always been linked to technology. Soon, artificial intelligence (AI) and computerized technology will revolutionize the efficiency and how we use greenhouses.

PHYSIOLOGICAL BENEFITS OF A GREENHOUSE

Did You Know?

Talking to your plants will help them grow. Plants love sounds, vibrations, and music. They are alive, after all.

In 2019, researchers determined that Americans' annual microplastic consumption ranges from 39,000 to 52,000 particles, depending on age and sex (Cox et al.), increasing to between 74,000 and 121,000 particles when inhalation is considered. This figure goes up an additional 90,000 particles annually for individuals who drink bottled water as their primary source of water, compared to an increase of 4,000 particles for people who consume only tap water (Cox et al.).

For the first time last year, scientists detected microplastics in "placental portions: maternal, fetal and amniochorial membranes" (Ragusa et al., 2021). The researchers warned that microplastics carry with them chemical substances that "could cause long-term effects on human health."

In a world that seems to have gone mad on harmful technological advancements, your greenhouse is an escape back into nature's welcoming and healing embrace.

For a self-sufficient individual like yourself who wants to grow your produce naturally and chemical-free, the greenhouse is the perfect method for doing so. Currently, the agricultural industry is deeply reliant on chemicals for food production. Industrial farmers regularly use organophosphate pesticides (e.g., chlorpyrifos, phosmet, methyl parathion, and azinphos-methyl) to control insects and other pests (EPA, 2015). Harvested crops sometimes contain residue from these pesticides. Unfortunately, research has shown an association between high consumption of organophosphate pesticides and childhood attention-deficit hyperactivity disorder(ADHD) (EPA, 2015). Other recent studies have reported associations between prenatal exposure to organophosphate pesticides and various neurodevelopmental deficits in childhood, some of which include reduced IQ, memory and perceptual reasoning (EPA, 2015).

Buying organic food is not a guarantee of it being chemical-free because chemicals from other sources of industrial production leak into our food. Perfluorochemicals used in food packaging before 2015 remain in today's environment where they can still be inhaled. According to the EPA (2015), some studies have found associations between prenatal exposure to perfluorochemicals and various adverse birth outcomes. Similarly, other chemicals used in food production, like Perchlorate, Polybrominated Diphenyl Ethers (PBDEs), and Bisphenol A (BPA), cause adverse health effects in the general population, especially the children.

Growing the fruit and vegetables you plan to consume, you control the chemicals introduced to your produce. When you serve a salad made from your greenhouse-grown lettuce and tomatoes, you can boldly attest that you know everything your produce has been through before it reached your plate. A greenhouse is a stimulating and educational hobby for people sick of buying chemically-enhanced fruits and vegetables.

Consuming home-grown organic food is, naturally, very healthy for you—as opposed to food grown with synthetic pesticides, harmful synthetic fertilizers, and antibiotics or growth hormones (The Lancet, 2017). In truth, organic supermarket food has attracted plenty of controversy since it gained popularity. Regulations surrounding organic food are too relaxed, and plenty of non-organic food is labeled organic. The US organic food market rose from less than $8 billion to more than 50 billion between 2000 and 2019 (Harvey & Rees, 2021). Yet, more than 100 fertilizers, pesticides, fungicides, and insecticides are used to produce organic food (Harvey & Rees, 2021).

There is no need for you to add toxins to your food with home-grown organic food. Your plants will thrive because of the care, love, and attention that you show towards them. Organic food has a higher level of nutrients, particularly polyphenols (Pendick, 2018). Some polyphenols are antioxidants that have anti-inflammatory and anti-cancer properties. Indeed, eating organic food can boost your antioxidant intake by up to 40% (Morello, 2014). Organic food also contains lower cadmium concentrations, a metal that can build up in the body and become toxic (Morello, 2014).

PSYCHOLOGICAL BENEFITS OF A GREENHOUSE

Did You Know?

There are over 10,000 varieties of tomatoes in the world. It is the world's most popular food.

In mental health, there is a field of study called "ecopsychology." Ecopsychology argues that exposure to the natural world has many beneficial effects, including reducing stress and promoting healing (Robbins, 2020). The English were correct to follow their desire to be closer to nature. Research into ecopsychology has now seen an uptake in the number of policymakers, employers, and healthcare providers who plan and conduct their human capital operations, focusing on the human need for nature.

A recent study by the European Centre for Environment & Human Health at the University of Exeter (White et al., 2019) found that doses of nature give people a sense of well-being and make them feel healthy. The study concluded that people who spend at least two hours a week in green spaces (defined as "local parks or other natural environments, either all at once or spaces over several visits") reported higher good-health and psychological well-being metrics, in contrast to those who spent less than two hours a week.

The study also concluded that the time spent in nature to receive these benefits had to reach two hours a week. Therefore, participants who spent even close to 119 minutes did not meet higher physiological and psychological well-being metrics. That is excellent news if you plan to own a greenhouse because you will exceed two hours every week. Nurturing plants is a labor-intensive affair that requires your love and devotion. You will be jubilant to know that the more time, resources, and energy you pour into your plants, the more they bless you in return. In essence, your care grows your plants, and your plants' growth improves your physical and mental well-being. Fundamentally, your greenhouse represents an ideal symbiotic relationship. Your plants give oxygen, and you take oxygen. You give CO2, and your plants take CO2. Your plants provide you with good health, and you give them life.

The study also concluded that the effects of nature on well-being do not discriminate but, instead, "cuts across different occupations, ethnic groups, people from rich and poor areas, and people with chronic illnesses and disabilities" (Robbins, 2020). These findings correspond to Ambrose et al. (2020), who similarly concluded that gardening makes people happy, regardless of race, gender, or socioeconomic class.

Why do people feel good when surrounded by Mother nature? The American Horticultural Therapy Association (2021) argues that the benefits of greenery on the human psyche and soul has been praised since ancient times. The non-profit organization of mental health professionals cites the examples of war veterans in the 1940s and 1950s who found significant healing in horticultural therapy. Simplistically, humans are wired to feel good amid nature. Be it animals, the snow, the sun, the forest, or the mountains, you will be hard-pressed to find someone who does not like at least one facet of nature.

Our love of nature stems from Mother Nature's natural healing and restorative powers. When we sense colors, textures, and fragrances; when we move our bodies to accommodate or tame nature; when we learn how to survive or tame the untamable wildness of nature, we are healing. We are renewing our minds and our bodies, strengthening the two things that make us who we are as humans. It is here that healing happens.

Essentially, as Robbins (2020) writes in the Yale School Of Environment, nature and the natural world is a human need, not a human want. Therefore, your decision to cultivate a greenhouse will be immensely beneficial to you, as this is a massive leap into also cultivating your mental well-being. One could argue that this decision was borne out of a deep need that must be fulfilled.

Time in nature is a stress antidote. It has been proven to lower blood pressure and stress hormone levels, among many other amazing psychological and physiological health benefits, such as:

- Speed up your rate of healing.
- Reduce nervous system arousal.
- Reduce attention deficit disorder.
- Reduce anxiety.
- Improve your mood.
- Reduce aggression.
- Enhance immune system function.
- Increase self-esteem.

A 2018 study titled. 'Gardening on a Psychiatric Inpatient Unit: Cultivating Recovery' confirms that spending time growing plants provides calmness and reduces feelings of isolation. It also stimulates a reflective process whereby participants use the garden as a symbol to gain insight into their illness" (Pieters et al., 2018).

PRACTICAL BENEFITS OF A GREENHOUSE

Did You Know?

There is a garden in England that grows 100 toxic, intoxicating, and narcotic plants. It is called The Alnwick Gardens, and it is only open to guided tours. Visitors are prohibited from smelling, touching, or tasting any plants. Despite this, some visitors have been known to faint from the plants' toxic fumes.

Your element of control remains one of the most significant benefits of the greenhouse. George Washington built his greenhouse to serve pineapple to his guests whenever he wanted to do so, and not only when in season. Most fruit and vegetables are seasonal; greenhouses allow you to bypass the rules of nature to produce fruit and vegetables anytime you desire by controlling the growing conditions. There are many ways to implement control in a greenhouse to maximize results.

1. Controlling the Weather

You have the power to control the weather inside your greenhouse. You can make it humid, cold, hot, or even drafty if required. For plants to grow outside of their natural season, you can mimic the ideal conditions by controlling the environment so that they thrive. This way, greenhouse gardeners can plant a variety of fruits and vegetables all year long.

The weather plays a significant part in whether or not plants survive. Your greenhouse will protect them from undesirable or extreme weather conditions. Any unseasonal temperature or seasonal changes, such as a snowy day in April or a summer drought, threaten your plants when you garden. Your greenhouse uses a translucent cover to shield your plants from this threat by defusing harsh sunshine and protecting them from heavy rainfall, allowing you to control their needs.

2. Protection

As discussed above, your greenhouse structure will protect your plants from the wind; a common problem with outdoor, open-air gardens is the destructive wind. With a sturdy well-anchored greenhouse, your plants will be protected.

Your structure also protects your plants from larger animals, such as neighborhood pets, nocturnal or woodland creatures, like deer, from wandering around in your garden and accidentally destroying the plants you worked hard to cultivate.

3. Pest Control

Unfortunately, you are not the only one interested in your garden. Squirrels, moles, birds, and smaller insects, like caterpillars, locusts, and mites, have a vested interest in your delicious plants. Pest control has been one of the greatest challenges to farmers and gardeners since agriculture began. Luckily, with a well-built structure, you can keep pesky bugs and animals that might tamper with your garden at bay.

Smaller pests, like rats, may still find their way into your greenhouse from time to time, but there are humane animal traps or even screens to help with this problem. Ultimately, this reduces the need for any toxic chemicals to keep pests out. A greenhouse assures you that you do not have to rely on toxic chemicals, like synthetic pesticides, to enjoy gardening. If you are cultivating food, you will also enjoy the opportunity to eat authentic organic food more frequently.

4. Multiple Plants

A greenhouse allows you the option to diversify what you want to grow. It keeps you on your toes because there are almost innumerable combinations of plants that you can grow in your greenhouse. The sun provides us with heat and light: two things that plants need to survive and thrive. The sun is free, so harnessing the tremendous energy of solar power is a very cost-effective, efficient, and sustainable way to garden.

5. Economical Costs

The beauty of the greenhouse is its versatility. Besides being a garden, you can store your gardening equipment and supplies. If you plant crops, you will also find that you are spending less money on fresh produce, which can be expensive, especially if you prefer organic.

A greenhouse helps you "shop without paying" for fresh organic produce within walking distance of your home. The cost of your greenhouse, gardening equipment and supplies will pay for themselves after a few years of gardening. Furthermore, you can extract the seeds from your produce and regrow plants cyclically. Nothing is wasted! The short-term expenses of choosing a greenhouse are worth the long-term benefits, be it the joy of interacting with plants and nature or the economic benefits of having your choice of fruit and vegetables without a need to buy from someone else.

6. Versatility

There is a greenhouse for everyone. If you want a small one, a big one, a simple one, an advanced one, you can find it all. Even better, some are easy to move and are customizable if you want to upgrade some of the functions like adding time-controlled bulbs for a specific plant or a new section for growing herbs.

You do not need technological or construction-savvy to build your greenhouse; most small to medium greenhouses are built using wood or lightweight aluminum. You can also use an easily installed and inexpensive gravel floor to keep your greenhouse dry and clean.

7. Health Benefits

We have already examined the fantastic benefits of gardening, so you can be sure that your greenhouse is an excellent investment for your health. Indeed, there are even more health benefits of growing your produce. Vegetables today contain 40% fewer nutrients than they did in the 1940s, thanks to what scientists call the 'dilution effect.' Fertilization and other aspects of industrialized farming have empowered us to produce quantity while forsaking quality.

Secondly, there is the 'genetic dilution effect.' This occurs when "plant breeders develop high-yielding varieties without a primary focus on broad nutrient content" (Long, 2009). You can choose crop breeds genetically high in nutrients and low in carbohydrates and sugars for your greenhouse.

The good news is that you can ditch industrialized farming processes and restore nutrients to your diet by growing your food. Likewise, growing your food means never having to worry about food recalls or the high possibility of eating cross-contaminated food. Keeping a clean, pest-free greenhouse is all the reassurance you need that your food is not contaminated.

There health benefits to having a greenhouse are too many to mention. So, get ready to destress, eat well, and even beat seasonal affective disorder (SAD)—thanks to the diffused lighting in greenhouses.

8. Self-sufficiency

Self-sufficiency is a human evolutionary trait. Humans have survived for generations by learning to rely on themselves for survival. Before agriculture took over as our primary mode of survival, we survived as a hunter-gatherer species. We foraged and hunted for food, surviving on our ability to produce hunting tools and spot nutritious, non-poisonous plants.

Our current agricultural age began 12,000 years ago thanks to climatic, environmental, and population changes worldwide. Nonetheless, humankind's adaptation to agriculture was its saving grace. Despite following a hunter-gatherer lifestyle for 200,000 years, the world population would not see exponential population growth until agriculture was introduced. Humans began to receive regular nutrients, unlike in their hunter-gatherer days, allowing them to live longer and become healthy enough to survive diseases they formerly couldn't. Put simply, agriculture increased the global human population from 4 million in 10,000 BCE to nearly 8 billion today (John Hopkins Center For A Livable Future, 2021).

The industrialization of agriculture removed many individuals from the farming lifestyle as our modern-day life became more reliant on supermarkets, gas stations, and restaurants for food. The popularity of self-sufficiency has grown in recent years, with many people choosing to learn how to grow their food.

In fact, research from the National Gardening Association (NGA) revealed that families involved in gardening rose by 200 percent between 2008 and 2013 (Garden, 2014). Thirty-five percent of households in the US now grow their food either in gardens at home or community gardens (Garden, 2014). The year 2013 saw higher household food garden participation and household spending on food gardens than the previous five years. Mike Metallo, President and CEO of the NGA, argues a food revolution is currently occurring in the US. An ever-increasing number of people, especially young people, are now growing their food (Garden, 2014). This growth has seen a spectacular jump in the past five years, shocking the gardening industry.

As humans move back to self-sustainability, access to fresh, healthy food becomes a bold act of self-love. This is especially noteworthy because of today's unstable economy, the rising costs of food (especially healthy, non-processed food), and the impact of climate change on global food production and distribution. Furthermore, the increasing frequency of natural disasters and pandemics has revealed the fragility of global food production and distribution networks. Consequently, individual farming is a great way to ensure you can thrive in today's unpredictable world.

Scientists, who previously referred to our changing world climate as a 'climate change,' now call this change a 'climate emergency.' There is no better time to improve self-sufficiency skills than, perhaps, during one of the biggest emergencies humankind has ever faced.

To make matters worse, the world population is rising at an exponential rate. It is set to increase to 10 billion by 2050. An article published recently (Lagomarsino, 2019) takes a daunting look at the future of our planet, specifically because humans are no longer knowledgeable on self-sufficiency. The rising population, along with the growing impact of climate change, means that learning how to nurture the perfect conditions to grow your own food is now an indispensable skill.

The article (Lagomarsino, 2019) states some worrying facts. For example, in 2019, an estimated 124 million people faced acute food shortages because of climate-related events, including flooding, irregular rains, high temperatures, and drought. As more and more regions worldwide begin to experience these climate change effects, food cultivation, agriculture and greenhouses will become one of the most essential things in human society and civilization.

Finally, self-sufficiency—even without a global disaster—enriches your life and the lives of those around you. In cases where you may produce more food than you need, you are also blessed with the option to preserve excess fruits and vegetables. This regular farming practice will prepare you for when you may lack access to the supermarkets for a considerable amount of time. Finally, you may find that you want to share some of your produce with neighbors. This is especially pertinent in the United States, where 16 million children suffer from hunger (Garden, 2014). A greenhouse provides self-sufficiency not just for you but for your neighborhood.

CHAPTER SUMMARY

- A greenhouse is a structure designed specifically to grow produce within regulated climatic conditions.
- You can precisely control your greenhouse environment to ensure maximum growth yield and quality of your plants. The element of control remains one of the greatest benefits of the greenhouse.
- Recorded history shows that greenhouses have a history dating back nearly two millennia.
- Artificial intelligence (AI) and computerized technology will revolutionize the efficiency and how we use greenhouses.
- Consuming produce grown in greenhouses means that you will consume less harmful chemicals proven to adversely affect humans.
- Gardening and surrounding yourself with nature is proven to promote mental health well-being.

In the next chapter, you will learn how to choose the type of greenhouse that is best for you.

CHAPTER TWO

Types of Greenhouses

"I must admit that when I first heard about it, I wasn't too excited about the idea of a greenhouse. I imagined the typical greenhouse, long, rectangular, with plastic walls and roof that let the sun through. Yes, I thought, this might extend the growing season, but it would mar her charming yard and diminish the charm of her huge, organic garden. Live and learn.

Jeri's greenhouse was, in fact, a little miracle, a small, glass-sided, light-filled jewel of a space where cherry tomatoes overflow their supports from spring through fall. It's more square than rectangular, with a deeply slanting glass roof, and—constructed of glass and wood with raised beds on either side as you walk it— creates a very special space that, to me, represents gardening at its most magical."

—Teo Spengler

There are many types of greenhouses on the market. Choosing one that works for you is a simple and straightforward process that you should not fret about. This chapter will help you to make the best choice for your greenhouse needs. Although there are many practical considerations when choosing your greenhouse, your emotional and mental consideration is the most important.

First and foremost, your greenhouse is a place of rest, healing, and life. You want to create a space that produces life, enhances healing, and promotes rest. You will spend a lot of time in this space, so you need to make it a 'home away from home.'

Your greenhouse is your sanctuary; it helps you to boost your mood and promotes emotional well-being. The simple fact is that you cannot feel these effects in a greenhouse that does not feel comfortable. That said, if you can construct a greenhouse that meets your needs as a gardener, then you have succeeded in creating a sanctuary for yourself.

Research has shown that gardening is associated with greater happiness for urban residents (Ambrose et al., 2020). Particularly illuminating was that the analysis revealed that gardeners do not feel the need for companionship when in their garden or greenhouse; they are perfectly content and happy to be alone with their plants.

Humans do not thrive in insufficient spaces. For example, "inadequate, poorly functioning and polluting infrastructure provisioning has been shown to have a significant impact on health outcomes, such as disease burden, and premature mortality" (Ambrose et al., 2020). Consider the spaces in which you typically feel most comfortable when choosing a greenhouse. Some prefer gardens because they can be outdoors, knee-deep in soil. Others prefer greenhouses because they offer the same gardening experience—albeit tidier.

Think about how you would like to use your garden before deciding which greenhouse would best suit your needs. Do you like small cozy spaces or big, open, airy spaces? Do you prefer tall shelves and an immaculate floor, or a cluttered floor and open walls? Will you enjoy your pet's companionship (if you have one) or to be alone? Would you like to set up a cozy corner for relaxation, reading, and even lunch inside your greenhouse?

WHAT TO CONSIDER BEFORE BUYING A GREENHOUSE

Careful consideration must be given to a few other practical things before choosing a greenhouse. Some solid research and writing down your greenhouse vision will help you avoid the beginner's mistake of making the wrong choice. A greenhouse should be a long-term purchase (except when you purchase a beginner's greenhouse), and making changes every few months can very quickly break the bank. Take as much care in researching as you would any other long-term purchases—like a car or a house. Planning is your safeguard against making any expensive mistakes.

There are four essential things to consider when planning or building your greenhouse:

1. What is My Usual Climate?
2. What Will I Grow and How Much?
3. Do I Need a Kit or a Hand-Built Greenhouse?
4. How Will My Space Reflect Me?

What is My Usual Climate?

Your climate will largely dictate the type of greenhouse you should consider. If you live in a colder region that sees regular ice and snow, you will need a well-insulated greenhouse; this is critical if you want to grow plants year-round. The best option, in this case, is a multiple-walled polycarbonate greenhouse. It comprises multiple layers filled with internal air spaces (either double or triple) that provide the insulation your plants need to survive the winter.

Or, you can consider twin-walled polyethylene, which insulates and provides a soft, diffused light that is of additional benefit to your plants. It is a great option that offers more flexibility than the more rigid multiple-walled polycarbonate. However, during the winter months, you will want to be prepared against snow accumulation, so carefully check the snow-load rating for the greenhouse model you wish to purchase. If you are building your greenhouse using your own material, make sure that it won't collapse under heavy snow. This could mean you use solid and sturdy wood and a well-built foundation.

If you are a gardener in a milder climate, you may need a greenhouse to house your plants when the weather is cold and uncertain. In this case, heavy-duty insulation may not be necessary, and you can opt for single-walled polycarbonate instead. Alternatively, you can use simple tempered glass panels; this is an excellent option because it lasts and won't degrade under the intensity of heavy sunlight.

You might want to avoid glass panels in very windy areas as it is fragile and may not survive long under heavy winds, hail, and storms. Woven polyethylene film lasts better under windy conditions because it is tougher. Twin-walled polyethylene or polycarbonate on a very sturdy frame will also hold up well under windy conditions. Keep all windows and doors in your greenhouse closed during a storm; this and your sturdy well-anchored foundation and frame will keep it standing in heavy wind and gales.

Like glass, polyethylene film is also fragile but is advantageous because of its low cost and easy setup. Nonetheless, it does not hold up well under strong winds or heavy weather conditions. Similarly, it does not withstand heavy sunlight well and degrades pretty quickly. Its low cost is a short-term advantage since you will need to replace every one to six years, especially after strong sunlight or heavy wind.

Some people will choose an attached greenhouse or an extension made onto your house to mitigate this risk. This option is much studier in extreme weather but comes with some disadvantages. Firstly, it can be challenging to control the temperature as it will always be affected by the temperature in your house. Secondly, the shade from your home might cause the greenhouse to receive less heat and sun rays. When your greenhouse is neither temperature nor light controlled, the ramifications to your plants cannot be understated. A free-standing greenhouse with a solid foundation might make more sense.

Finally, if you live in a cold climate and want a glass greenhouse, you must consider insulation. Choose a glass with a heat-retaining coat, such as "low-E."

Low-E means "low emissivity." The surface of a particular material emits low levels of radiant thermal energy, and glass generally emits heat as quickly as it receives it. Indeed, you can choose to heat your greenhouse more often, but without proper insulation, this will become too costly. Low-E glass will keep emissivity low, allowing for good insulation all year round. Twin-walled polyethylene has the best low-E of any greenhouse glazing.

To make things simpler, you can figure out your USDA plant hardiness zone. This is the standard through which you can determine which plants will most likely thrive in your region. If citrus plants can thrive in your area – for example, lemons thrive in Florida – you can use this information to decide what greenhouse conditions are best for a lemon tree. The USDA Plant Hardiness Zone Map is based on the average annual minimum winter temperature. It is divided into 10-degree Fahrenheit zones.

What Will I Grow and How Much?

What do you plan on growing? Do you want to grow flowers and plants or substantial quantities of fruits and vegetables? If you are growing plants, will you be raising big plants or small plants? When growing produce, do you mean to grow big produce, like yams and pumpkins, or smaller ones like tomatoes and lemons? Or, perhaps you intend to grow both produce and plants? The type and number of plants you want to grow will determine the type of greenhouse you need.

Most experienced gardeners will tell you that their planting purchases are getting out of hand. Your love of gardening and your joy of seeing plants grow - make you a great gardener. You might think that you only need a small greenhouse only to regret this afterward. Of course, you would need to consider your available space before erecting a greenhouse. It might be a more prudent option to buy a slightly larger greenhouse than what you need if you have the space. That way, if you feel any desire to add more plants, you can do so.

Be prudent with the space and size of your greenhouse, and carefully consider the practicalities of your decision. Do not rush; it is better to wait and ultimately make the right purchase than rush into a decision you may regret. It can become costly to change your greenhouse multiple times to accommodate your needs.

As a beginner, you may want to try a starter greenhouse. You only need a potting bench, soil, and your plants or seeds with a starter greenhouse. You could consider a cold frame, a box that you can move from one garden bed to another to protect your plants from frost. A portable garden cloche is another option as a starter greenhouse. These options are inexpensive, require no permit, and allow you to experiment with gardening in a controlled environment without the expense of building a greenhouse. After using these tools, you may decide that you are ready for a walk-in greenhouse.

Then again, if you are an experienced gardener branching into greenhouse gardening for the first time, you may have different needs. In this case, you may want to 'go bigger' and begin growing plants that need more complex, often year-round care. Thus, you will need a roomier "grower" greenhouse.

Greenhouses come in many different shapes and sizes. They range from the compact, smaller sizes (4'x6' footprint) to the medium sizes (10'x12' footprint) and finally to the larger scale size big enough for commercial gardening (20'x16' footprint). A medium-sized greenhouse of 6'x8' or 8'x10' is usually perfect for the needs of any amateur or experienced gardener. You will need to ensure that you have the space to move around in your greenhouse.

An average greenhouse measures 7ft in height. However, you can buy or build a higher greenhouse, but it will require more heating because hot air rises. Unless you need the extra height for the sake of growing taller plants, there is no need for this.

Do I Need a Kit or a Hand-Built Greenhouse?

Most people prefer to use greenhouse kits. These kits require assembly—usually by two people. Think of it as a more extensive, slightly more complicated Ikea furniture installation. You will have an easier time if you study the components, parts, and instructions before attempting to put it up.

You can also opt to build your greenhouse. In this instance, most people choose to hire a builder or get some assistance from someone with building experience. You don't need building experience to attempt to build one yourself. But, you will need to do a lot of research to ensure that you are fully prepared. Ask as many questions as you can about the tools and methods required.

Reputable greenhouse manufacturers offer good technical advice and support to help you along the way.

Building your greenhouse requires as much meticulous planning as choosing your greenhouse; it is a structure that will need to last for a long time. It will hold a lot, if not all, of your plants, gardening tools, equipment, seeds, and more. Economically, this structure will contain a significant financial investment. You won't park a Porsche in a garage made of bamboo sticks. Take your time to plan every detail of your greenhouse. What are the exact measurements? Who is the local supplier, and do they have it in stock? There is no point in hiring a builder to construct your greenhouse if the metal frames you require are unavailable.

Before making your purchase, research the company, its practices and policies extensively. This is your guarantee that you will receive a good product and good service. Research the legalities and practicalities of purchasing from this company, including the warranty period and shipping information. How long before your items are shipped and the expected time of delivery. What are the shipping and logistics insurance costs?

Additionally, you want to make sure that the company you buy from has a reputation for good service and products. Try to find reviews online, or ask on internet forums devoted to gardening and greenhouses. You need to know what kind of technical assistance will be available pre-purchase, during purchase, and post-purchase. Is assistance available on weekends for any installation questions?

Gardeners love to share tips and expert advice, so do not be afraid to reach out. If there are no gardeners or gardening clubs around you, the internet is a fantastic resource to find other gardeners from all around the world. One such resource exists on our Facebook page as www.facebook.com/groups/greenhousegardeners.

How Will My Space Reflect Me?

You will want the space encapsulating your hobby to reflect you. Even if you don't plan this aspect, you will find that your space will slowly begin to morph to reflect traces of who you are. Nonetheless, if you want your greenhouse to feel like home, there are ways to make the space reflect you. You will want to craft the area inside and around your greenhouse to beautify it. After all, a gardener's job is as much about cultivating nature's beauty as her bounty. Think about it this way: Plants can pick up on your emotional energy; if you are in a space that causes you to feel relaxed and happy, your plants pick up on it and feel relaxed, too, helping them to grow even better and faster.

When researching your greenhouse, incorporate research on how to decorate it. What theme do you want? Do you want an antique theme or, perhaps, a light, airy theme created using fairy lights, floral chairs, and colorful planters? You will spend a lot of time in your greenhouse, so make it suit your tastes. Perhaps you will be planting herbs and want others to enjoy the wonderfully therapeutic fragrances from your mint, rosemary, and thyme plants? In this case, a small garden table and a couple of chairs might lure your friends and family to sit with you.

Another thing to consider is how to decorate the outside of your greenhouse. Most people place their greenhouse in their garden, where you may already grow beautiful plants and flowers that compliment the shiny glass of your greenhouse. If not, you can plant a few flowers to add more color and excitement to the surrounding area. You should also consider whether to pave or gravel the walk from your home to your greenhouse. Constant walking to and from the greenhouse may wear down the grass, causing it to look decrepit in an otherwise glorious space. Ensure you have an area inside your greenhouse to store your tools and equipment neatly and tidily. You may want to install a shelf or a cupboard for this purpose. Leaving your tools and equipment lying around inside or outside your greenhouse will cause you stress, thereby defeating the purpose of creating a relaxing environment.

WHICH GREENHOUSE SHOULD I CHOOSE?

Once you have pored through all the considerations of a greenhouse purchase, you are ready to buy or build one. Your decisions concerning the material, glass, size, heating, insulation, location and many more will inform your choice about which greenhouse to build or buy. There are a few different types to consider.

1. Lean-To Greenhouse

   The Lean-To Greenhouse, also known as an Attached Greenhouse, is placed against the side of the building, i.e., *leaned to* the building. It is compact-sized and does not necessarily have to be attached to your home; it can be attached to your garage or shed, for example.

   Advantages

   This type of greenhouse is perfect if you have limited space in your surroundings. It makes excellent use of space and saves material by using an already-existing wall of a building. Since one wall is against a building, lean-to greenhouses retain heat much better than stand-alone greenhouses. Being placed right next to your house eliminates the need for long walks and places it right next to amenities, such as heating, light, and water. You can use your lean-to greenhouse to grow plants or start seeds on benches. The lean-to greenhouse can be very aesthetic and adds a new dimension of landscaping beauty to your home.

   Disadvantages

   The lean-to greenhouse loses a quarter of its heat and light source by sharing an existing wall. Greenhouses use heat- and light-penetrable material so that plants can be insulated and photosynthesized to grow. As a result, your plants may not get adequate light depending on the position of your building in relation to the greenhouse. The height of your load-bearing wall also limits you in terms of size; you may be forced to buy a tiny lean-to greenhouse. The higher the wall, the wider your lean-to greenhouse can be.

As with everything in life, the more efficient and high-quality you want your lean-to greenhouse to be, the more it will cost. You can purchase lean-to greenhouse kits, but these are rarer to find than the other options. Should you decide to build your lean-to greenhouse or pay a builder to build one for you, you will have to consider the material carefully. You will need a sturdy material for the base as if the lean-to greenhouse is not sturdy, it can damage the building should it collapse under bad weather. Consider using wood or brick for your base building construction, which will last longer and look more aesthetically pleasing.

Is This Greenhouse Right for Me?

A lean-to greenhouse can be an efficient and economical purchase. If it meets your needs, you will enjoy your new structure immensely. You may need to apply for zoning permissions depending on the local rules of your area and the size and classification of your lean-to greenhouse.

The lean-to greenhouse may need supplementary heating during colder periods, so you will want to consider if you can provide enough heat from a supplementary source. If you live in an area with a lot of snow, you cannot use glass windows because snow breaks glass easily. You will have to select a lean-to greenhouse made with polycarbonate. In warmer weather, lean-to greenhouses are prone to overheating because the solid wall side makes it harder for you to control the temperature.

2. Ridge and Furrow Greenhouse
   Also known as gutter-connected greenhouses, as the name suggests, the ridge and furrow greenhouse is built by joining even-span structures (sometimes called A-frame structures) with multiple ridges in a neat row. Each row is connected at the eave, with gutters at the base of each adjoining eave, allowing for excess snow and rain to drain off. The roof of a ridge and furrow greenhouse usually makes an A shape or curved arches.

The arched roof must be covered with light materials, such as polyethylene or polycarbonates, while the body can withstand heavier materials, like fiberglass or glass.

Advantages

The ridge and furrow connection is the most popular greenhouse because it gives the gardener enough room to grow many plants. It is very efficient because it saves on automation and energy by consolidating the space and resources inside the greenhouse. There is no need to divide plants into sections (based on their climate or water needs), making it easier to maintain the heat in the greenhouse since the entire unit receives the same amount and level of heat. With fewer windows and doors, the heat stays in. Indeed, the connected greenhouses are very economical because they allow for more light and heat penetration from the sun.

The ridge and furrow greenhouse can be extended without building or purchasing a whole new greenhouse, making it more economical in the long term.

There is plenty of space within each gutter-connected greenhouse to install heating systems, electrical connections, and water hookups. The connected greenhouses also mean that, should you need to expand the climate-control system in your greenhouse, this can be accomplished at little cost if you have already installed utilities in one unit.

Disadvantages

The gutter-connected greenhouse is effective in most environments, but you will need to be more watchful in colder climates. When it snows, the additional load on the structure can cause damage, so consider this when constructing the greenhouse. You will want to create furrows that do not accumulate too much snow but are strong enough to withstand the additional load. Unlike a traditionally sloped greenhouse, where snow slides off, the snow remains within the furrow unless you remove it or it melts. You must install the gutters correctly, as failure here will cause water build-up in the furrows. This can damage the structure or cast a shadow, limiting the sunlight, causing your plants to die.

Is This Greenhouse Right for Me?

This greenhouse is suitable if you have a big piece of land and plan to have a giant greenhouse filled with many plants; however, it is costly to set up.

3. Hoop House

Curved like half a hoop, as its name suggests, the hoop house is constructed using either aluminum or plastic PVC pipes. The pipes form the structure of the hoop, which is then covered with polymer plastic sheeting. A double layer of the sheeting can be used for added insulation.

Unlike most greenhouses, it is recommended to install the hoop house close to the shade of a tree in warmer climates. This gives plants added shaded during the hottest parts of the day and prevents them from dying. Like all greenhouses, however, the hoop house must be south-facing. If you live further north, where the climate is colder and need less shade for your plants. In this case, you will need to keep any neighboring structures on the northern side of the hoop house to help retain heat and block the wind.

Advantages

The hoop house is for the horticulturist on a budget. It can cost less than $1 per square meter to install because it is easier to build. The hoop house comes in different sizes and can be erected by two or three people in a matter of days. The materials used to create a hoop house are widely available in garden supply and home improvement stores. Although the material used to construct a hoop house is not as durable as glass or polyethylene, a well-built greenhouse of this kind can withstand even heavy wind and rain with very little damage. During the winter, the half-hoop shape of its roof disallows snow and ice from building up on the plastic, minimizing damage in the process.

Disadvantages

There are very few ways to control the climate in a hoop house. Adding heating systems or electricity would be inconvenient and dangerous. Gardeners who use hoop houses must control the temperature and climate using natural means. The doors are kept shut in cold weather and left open in warm weather. Inserting shade cloth between the poles and plastic during mid-summer can prevent your crops from overheating.

Is This Greenhouse Right for Me?

The hoop house is an excellent start if you are undecided about investing in a greenhouse. They don't require a concrete pad like most greenhouses, and they can be quickly demolished, upgraded, or extended with little effort.

4. Even Span Greenhouse

   An even span greenhouse is constructed with two evenly-measured sloping roofs. You can build an even span greenhouse as a free-standing unit or attached to an existing building. When attached, the even span greenhouse is differentiated from a lean-to greenhouse because it retains its entire symmetrical roof.

   Advantages

   The even span greenhouse is one of the most popular greenhouses because it is among the easiest to construct. The design is very efficient, as it allows for plenty of space for plants and the gardener and is also very aesthetically pleasing—particularly the ones with curved eaves. Its main economic characteristic is the wide availability of a prefabricated kit.

   There is transparent material on all sides of this greenhouse, giving your plants plenty of light. The uniform shape also brings uniform heating, and the A-shape of the roof prevents rain and snow from accumulating, damaging the structure or the plants. Likewise, you can construct yours to be as big or as small as you choose.

   Disadvantages

The even span greenhouse is expensive to set up. Moreover, having all sides transparent means that it needs its own heating system, especially during colder months.

5. Uneven Span Greenhouse

The opposite of the even span greenhouse, the uneven span greenhouse has one roof slope longer than the other. This model is often used when a gardener wants to place a greenhouse on a hill or a sloped surface. In other circumstances, it is used when a gardener wants to take advantage of solar angles.

When building an uneven span greenhouse, the roof is not made equal either in width or pitch. The steeper angle is constructed to face the south - the direction of the sun. Furthermore, the side facing the south side is transparent, while the opposing side facing the north is opaque to conserve energy. This type of greenhouse has decreased in popularity, possibly because urbanization, farming, and human dispersion have changed land terrain. Essentially, most people don't live in very hilly areas unless they are urbanized.

Advantages

The most significant advantage of this greenhouse is that it works well when used on hillsides, allowing plenty of sunlight.

Disadvantages

It is difficult to find specialized equipment for this type of greenhouse. You would also find it near impossible or very expensive to expand the uneven span greenhouse. The uneven span greenhouse is very costly relative to a hoop house or an even-span greenhouse. Typically, the roof needs a lot of support and maintenance, adding to the cost. This greenhouse's advantage becomes a disadvantage in regions closer to the equator because it allows too much light and heat in, killing your plants.

GREENHOUSE MATERIALS

Your greenhouse frame will typically be made out of wood, aluminum, or steel.

The least expensive is aluminum, which happens to be the most durable, making it the most widely used choice. Aluminum is easy to form into various shapes and thicknesses, making it the perfect material for building greenhouses of all shapes and sizes. Conversely, steel is quite heavy and is used for framing glass panels. Wood can be durable if used correctly. Ensure you use pressure-treated lumber that will resist decay in a moist environment and non-toxic lumber because the constant heat in the greenhouse may cause the toxins to release into the atmosphere, poisoning your plants.

- There are many types of greenhouses on the market. Choosing one that works for you is very important.
- Careful consideration, solid research, and writing down your vision for your greenhouse will help you avoid the beginner's mistake of choosing the wrong greenhouse.
- Your area will also dictate what type of greenhouse you can buy.
- Ensure you have a space inside your greenhouse to store all your tools and equipment neatly and tidily. You may want to install a shelf or a cupboard that keeps everything neatly put away.
- It is better to wait and make the right purchase than to rush into a decision that you may regret.
- One long side of your greenhouse should ideally be facing the south. This allows for the sun to run along the length of it during the day.
- Do not neglect the beauty of your greenhouse and its surroundings.
- You must research local zoning regulations before erecting a greenhouse.

In the next chapter, you will learn how to create the optimal conditions needed to ensure your greenhouse is functioning and efficient.

CHAPTER THREE

Cultivating an Efficient Greenhouse

"We may think that we are nurturing our garden, but of course, it's our garden
that is really nurturing us."

–Jenny Uglow

In a world on the brink of overpopulation combined with the disastrous effects of climate change, learning how to create the perfect conditions for gardening is a critical skill, one that our survival could depend on for the next few centuries. Congratulations! You are making a headstart on the very skill needed to survive on this planet.

Industrial agriculture has removed us entirely from the agricultural process, sterilizing us from the realities of life and growth on Planet Earth. Previously these skills were passed from generation to generation; now, most of us have to learn this as adults—trying to gather as much information from as many sources as possible. Undeniably, one of the most critical skills to learn for greenhouse gardening is how to create the perfect conditions for your plants to thrive. There is no point in investing in the best greenhouse and stocking up on the best tools and seeds if all your plants are going to die. This chapter will teach you how to create the optimal condition for plant excellence.

Creating the perfect conditions for your plants to thrive is an ongoing process that must remain consistent. Both outdoor and greenhouse gardening is the science of creating and nurturing life. Just like growing a baby during pregnancy or healing a sick patient in the hospital, life needs constant care to survive and thrive. In your greenhouse, you will have to consciously consider the many measures needed to keep your soil and plants consistently healthy. These measures relate to location, water, and drainage.

LOCATION

Did You Know?

Children who grow their food are more likely to eat fresh fruits and vegetables.

- Where Will I Position My Greenhouse?

One long side of your greenhouse should ideally face south. This allows the sun to run along the length of it during the day. A greenhouse is made up mostly of glass or clear plastic specifically to collect light and heat energy from the sun in the daytime to allow your plants to thrive. Therefore, placing your greenhouse in deep shade, or surrounded by trees, is not a good idea.

Distance is a crucial factor in the location of your greenhouse. You should consider the distance of your greenhouse from the water and electricity supply because running long wires and pipes is not ideal. The ventilation needs of your greenhouse are also crucial; therefore, the direction of the wind must be considered when planning the position of your greenhouse to ensure that your plants get enough CO2.

Additionally, you should ensure that the ground is level. If the ground has any slants, slopes, or ramps, this can cause drained water to stagnate. It can also be a hazard causing trips and falls in an already compact space.

- Do I have Any Restrictions?

There are many restrictions to consider for your new greenhouse. We have discussed the size and location, now we must consider the visual impact. As a gardener, your hobby lies in natural beauty; you are attracted to horticulture because it gives so much beauty to the world. Likewise, you must not sacrifice beauty when considering a greenhouse. Once you have chosen your location, visualize your greenhouse; does it enhance the area? How will it visually impact the surrounding area? Will it blend in or stick out jaggedly, detracting from the area's beauty? If you have neighbors, you must consider their view, as they might not be too happy seeing an unattractive structure ruining the visual experiences of their space.

You will have to look at your greenhouse and its surrounding areas daily, and you should feel joy when doing so. Think of it as your greenhouse nourishing your emotional and spiritual wellbeing not just through the act of gardening itself but also through visual nourishment. To achieve this, choose a greenhouse that appeals to your aesthetic style. Do you prefer the smooth, clean lines of a glass greenhouse? Or, do you want a green greenhouse that visually represents the vegetation it encapsulates?

You can also carry out landscaping in the areas surrounding your greenhouse to elevate the aesthetics, making it look more welcoming, like a home.

Finally, you must research local zoning regulations for your area. You may need permission from different authorities before you can erect a greenhouse, especially if it is a medium or large greenhouse. For an attached greenhouse, you may need zoning permission; research the legal requirements. That way, you can purchase a greenhouse that meets these requirements. Some zoning permissions also require a leveled footprint and evidence of good drainage. Be prepared.

WATER

Of course, you will need proper irrigation for your greenhouse. Your plants need water; that's a no-brainer. An irrigation system is a watering process that you choose for your plants. Whether you decide to have timed-water releases or water your plants through a simple hose, it all counts as irrigation. There are a few irrigation systems to consider, depending on how your greenhouse is organized. Usually, the irrigation should keep watering the plants even when you're away; alternatively, you may choose to hand-water your plants. Hand-watering can be tiring; an irrigation system helps take the burden off your shoulders so that you don't have to visit the greenhouse as much to water your plants.

Capillary mats are an option. It is a sub-irrigation system that slowly but regularly waters your plants. Mats that slowly ooze water are placed under your pots and flats; the plant soaks this up through the drip holes underneath. The plant will not soak up any excess water. Instead, it is collected in plastic liners or a flood floor to be reused. This system is advantageous because it allows your plants to take in as much water as they need without being overwatered. Unquestionably, overwatering a plant will very likely lead to rot and fungal disease, a consequence that must be avoided at all costs. (Elliott et al., 2019)

Another option is a flood floor. Waterproof (or integral) concrete is generally best for constructing a flood floor; however, standard concrete can be coated to enhance its natural resistance to water. The concrete surface of this flood floor is expertly smoothed, allowing very little water to remain on the surface after a watering cycle. Traditionally, flood floors are pitched upward from the center to the edge to encourage drainage. The edge is typically an inch or two higher than the center, forming a shallow "V." At the base of the "V," holes are then drilled into the concrete to the supply and return line allowing water to flow in a continuous cycle. It is more cost-effective than the bench system as it eliminates a substantial amount of plumbing. (Elliott et al., 2019)

It takes 5 to 10 minutes for the flood floor to fill up, with drainage taking a few more minutes. The greater the depth of the irrigation head, the longer it takes to drain. Recent innovations have seen the "V"-shaped flood floors replaced with a "W"-shape; that fills and drains much faster. The "W"-shape has a row of fill and drain ports at each low point in the "W," giving a shorter run from the high to the low. The conventional system runs at about 20 minutes per ebb and flow cycle compared to the new system, which can complete a cycle in under five minutes. The enhanced speed of this system reduces the likelihood of your plants becoming overly saturated, which in turn reduces the likelihood of developing and spreading root-borne pathogens through the irrigation process. The rapid ebb and flow watering also offers better efficiency with water and fertilizer use. (Elliott et al., 2019)

The drip greenhouse irrigation system is constructed as a network of tubes and spray heads connected to the base water source. It is a perfect system because not all plants have the same water requirements. The tubes travel along the length of your greenhouse to each plant with spray heads selected depending on their exact water needs. (Elliott et al., 2019)

Drip irrigation is a controlled method for keeping your plants watered without running the risk of under or over-watering. The drip irrigation system is simple and allows water to reach each plant based on individual needs. The water reaches every pot and flat in your greenhouse based on your timer and flow gauge settings. It is inexpensive, easy to use, and easy to maintain. You can easily remove or add micro-tubing as and when needed. (Elliott et al., 2019)

DRAINAGE

As a new greenhouse owner, proper drainage is a vital aspect to consider. With tons of water sprayed onto your plants, you will most likely encounter water on the floor and water getting onto other plants when it's not their time to be watered. A simple drainage system, usually with greenhouse gutters, drain pipes, or swales, can help reuse this water.

If you do not plan for proper drainage in your greenhouse, it will create problems inside and outside. Accidents are very likely when working on a wet floor, and it can cause diseases for your plants. You should also effectively handle the rain and surface water around your greenhouse to avoid erosion and flooding.

Inside Drainage

If you do not use a concrete floor, a 6- to 8-inch gravel or stone base under the floor acts as the collection area for any excess water. Not only will gravel save on construction costs, but it also prevents any infections and weeds from multiplying. Your walkway will make pushing carts simpler and should always be sloped slightly to one side for additional drainage.

Full concrete floors are the best choice. They are solid, long-lasting, and need very little maintenance. Still, you should slightly slope the concrete floors too. Professor John Bartok, Jr., an agricultural engineer and extension professor emeritus in the Natural Resource Management and Engineering Department at the University of Connecticut, writing for Greenhouse Product News (Bartok Jr., 2007), explains the technicalities of constructing a full concrete floor. He advises creating a slope of 1/8-inch per linear foot (or 1 inch per 8 feet). According to him, this is the standard, even if it is more expensive. You should also construct a trench drain along the sidewalls or post lines of your greenhouse. This will make the installation of the greenhouse floor much more manageable and allow for quicker floor drainage. Today, most trench drains are made of polyethylene and manufactured with anchor tables to be attached to the concrete.

If you have a small greenhouse, the drainage may lead to a dry well. A dry well is an underground structure that accumulates surface runoff water from rain, greenhouses, or gardening and slowly allows the water to soak back into the ground, dissipating back into the groundwater. This is substantially preferable to allowing excess water to flow into your neighbor's property, which may also be against the law depending on the restrictions and regulations in your region. Be sure you are familiar with these rules.

If you have a giant greenhouse, your drains should be connected, ultimately leading to daylight. Suppose your greenhouse rests in an aquifer area. In that case, local regulations may dictate the floor water is collected in a sump (a pit specifically designed to collect undesirable liquids, such as drainage or chemical-infused water.) You might also need to install a vinyl liner below the floor of your greenhouse to stop fertilizers and pesticides from entering local natural water supplies.

If you recall, the previous chapter briefly discussed considerations to be made concerning roof drainage; it is becoming a massive consideration as greenhouses become larger and larger. Previously, this water would run off and become groundwater; now, roof drainage is being captured for reuse. With drainage, greenhouse gardening becomes very technical, and your design is dependent on the area in which you live. According to Professor Bartok Jr. (2007), this drainage design must consider the rainfall, storms, hurricanes, and wet weather the region sees.

Curtain Drain

A curtain drain may be needed to lower the water table around the greenhouse or intercept water flowing from a slope. This usually occurs wherever there is an impermeable soil layer below ground level. Rainwater percolates through the topsoil to the hardpan layer before traveling laterally to reach daylight. (Bartok Jr., 2007)

To construct a curtain drain, dig a trench until you reach the impermeable soil layer. Place geotextile in the trench, along with a perforated drainpipe, placed on 3-6 inches of gravel or pea stone before backfilling the trench with gravel or stone. To avoid the risk of collapse in trenches over 4 ft deep, use shoring—a method whereby a structure at risk of collapse is temporarily supported using shores. Your drainpipe should be sloped about 1/8-inch per foot to a detention pond or grade.

Designing Your Drainage System

Everything in your greenhouse that can collect water must be designed to handle runoff, including gutters, drain pipes, downspouts, and swales. Should you wish, you can design your greenhouse to allow any water collected in the gutters to run off into a swale (a form of urban drainage). Nonetheless, a more popular system among greenhouse enthusiasts is a piping system that collects drained water and directs it to a pond or drainage area. The technicalities of the piping system (Bartok Jr., 2007) are as follows:

Downspouts are erected to carry the water to lateral pipes connected to a larger main pipe. You should place these downspouts about 50 ft. apart along the gutter. You don't want to space them too far apart to avoid water flowing over the gutter and into the greenhouse.

Ensure your piping system is sufficiently sized to handle the volume of water collected. This would mean that a 6-inch lateral drain is adequate to collect the water from a gutter downspout that drains a 25 x 100-ft. section of roof, but only if the slope of the pipe is 6 inches in 100 ft. If a lateral pipe is needed to drain eight of the previously mentioned sections, it would have to be a 10-inch lateral pipe if the same slope is used (8 sections x 2,500 sq. ft. per section = 20,000 sq.ft.). (Bartok Jr., 2007)

Grass or stone-covered swales are typically used to drain the space between the greenhouses. The area should be graded into a V-shape. After grading, the sides must have a vertical-to-horizontal slope of between 1 and 5-ft. The bottom of the V must slope toward one or both ends of the greenhouse, depending on where the water will be discharged. For larger installations of more than one greenhouse, you might find it easier to install a catch basin at the end of each greenhouse before carrying the water in a below-ground piping system. (Bartok Jr., 2007)

Benefits of Detention Ponds

A detention pond is a greenhouse control structure that collects substantial volumes of water before slowly releasing it over several days—the sedimentation in this process allows organic matter and other pollutants to settle out before release. Detention ponds prevent runoff to curtain drains, keep drained water away from paved areas, and keep the greenhouse roof from flooding a neighboring property.

A detention pond must be designed by an engineer who will consider the area from which the water will be collected, the peak flow rate, the soil type in the area, and the permissible discharge rate. An adept engineer will also calculate for an emergency spillway to handle storms that may exceed the design flow. Detention ponds usually cost around $1 per cubic ft. of storage capacity. They should be fenced off to prevent animals from being attracted to your greenhouse and causing a nuisance. Expecting a deer not to be enticed by the vegetation in your greenhouse is futile.

The pond is often dry between storms.

Governmental Regulations

There are several governmental regulations to take into account when building your drainage system. It is your responsibility to carefully plan for all water to be collected or drained adequately. We will discuss later in this chapter how to set up a greenhouse drainage system to reuse water, thus avoiding any runoff into the neighboring properties. It may be necessary to hire an engineer to check that downstream waterways and road culverts are large enough to handle any excess water from your greenhouse. You cannot assume that it is okay for the excess water to wash into a swamp or lake just because it is clean water; in most cases, you will need a permit for this water discharge.

If you live in an area that follows zoning regulations, your engineer must create a plot plan showing the proposed location and draining measures of your greenhouse. Do your research carefully because these laws are all based on local regulations.

Today there is a renewed interest in growing plants hydroponically. Hydroponics, dating back to 600 BCE, is growing plants in nutrient fortified water rather than soil. A Harvard University published article (Lagomarsino,

2019) explains the origins. The method was developed in the 19th century after the German botanist Julius Sachs spent his entire career researching the essential elements needed for plants to survive. After carefully researching the differences between plants grown in soil and those grown in water, the University of Wurzburg botanist discovered that soil is not a requirement for plant life, but rather the nutrients derived from the microorganisms that live in the soil. After many more years of research, Sachs published the "nutrient solution," a formula for growing plants in water. This was the beginning of hydroponic technology and research.

Today, experimental horticulturists can now purchase hydroponic greenhouses. These cost less since they use less soil (of course) and less water. Plants grown in hydroponic greenhouses generally grow 30% faster than those grown in soil greenhouses. The hydroponic greenhouses produce ten times more yield than soil greenhouses. It is no wonder agriculturalists believe it to be the future of food production for the world's ever-increasing population (Lagomarsino, 2019). To find out more about hydroponic agriculture, visit https://www.nal.usda.gov/afsic/hydroponics.

DON'T WATER YOUR ANXIETY

Did You Know?

One U.S. farm feeds 166 people annually in the U.S. and abroad. The global population is expected to increase by 2.2 billion by 2050, which means the world's farmers will have to increase food production by 70%.

Although you control the conditions in your greenhouse, do not despair if everything does not fall into place immediately. Creating the perfect conditions for a greenhouse can be very technical, sometimes technical enough to require an engineer's expertise.

Greenhouse gardening is like cooking or starting a new job. Expect errors as a beginner and then expect more errors as you become an expert.

You can control the conditions within your greenhouse, but that is not always guaranteed in cases of extreme weather. The most loving thing you can do for your plants is creating consistent optimal conditions to make them happy; however, learning this will take time, especially if you are a greenhouse beginner. Sometimes you may fail, but that's a natural consequence of learning a new task. It simply means you are one step closer to expertise.

CHAPTER SUMMARY

- In today's world, learning how to nurture the perfect conditions for gardening is an indispensable skill.
- Proper irrigation is vital for every greenhouse.
- A simple drainage system can help you reuse any lost water.
- Without proper drainage in your greenhouse, it will begin to create problems both inside and out.
- You may need an engineer to assist in designing your drainage pond.
- Although you control the conditions in your greenhouse, do not despair if everything does not fall into place immediately.
- Expect errors as a beginner and expect more errors as you become an expert.
- Creating consistent optimal conditions for your plants is the most loving thing you can do for them.

In the next chapter, you will learn the importance of the greenhouse environment to keep your plants thriving.

CHAPTER FOUR

Keeping My Plants Alive

"Odd as I am sure it will appear to some, I can think of no better form of personal involvement in the cure of the environment than that of gardening. A person who is growing a garden, if he is growing it organically, is improving a piece of the world. He is producing something to eat, which makes him somewhat independent of the grocery business, but he is also enlarging, for himself, the meaning of food and the pleasure of eating."

—Wendell Berry

One of the most vital conditions to keep in mind for your plants' well-being is the "weather" inside your greenhouse. Plants are dependent on air, water, soil, sunlight, and moderate weather conditions to survive. If their surroundings are extreme, your plants may die, barely grow, or grow with deformities. While all plants have different optimal temperatures for thriving, most plants need warmth to survive as a general concept.

Four variables control the weather conditions within your greenhouse. They are:

1. Heating
2. Ventilation
3. Shade
4. Humidity

HEATING

Greenhouse temperatures are usually set at around 80 to 85 degrees Fahrenheit (about 26 to 29 degrees Celsius). Hence, it is imperative to learn how to maintain the temperature within your greenhouse. The purpose of a greenhouse is to keep your plants warm all year round using the sun's superb heating power.

While the sun may heat your greenhouse naturally, you may still need some type of heating system to ensure the temperature is steady all year round. An "unheated greenhouse" uses only direct solar energy. If you live in a warmer climate, you may rarely need to warm your greenhouse; your challenge may be to ventilate and cool your greenhouse. Nevertheless, there are other systems you can employ to heat your greenhouse artificially when the sun is not strong enough or during colder months. There are four ways to artificially heat your greenhouse. These are:

- Electric Heaters
- Gas Heaters

- Wood Stove
- Kerosene Heaters

Electric Heaters

Using an electric heater is inexpensive as you may only need to keep it on for a few hours on extra cold nights. After this, the heat will be insulated inside the greenhouse for many hours. You can set your electric heater on an automatic timer or thermostat to automate the process. Today's electric heaters are very safe with an automatic shut-off feature if it falls or gets too hot.

Gas Heaters

A gas heater burns fuel to keep your plants warm, with the unfortunate side effect of producing carbon monoxide. It comes with a further complication because it uses up the oxygen in your greenhouse—oxygen that your plants need for survival. You may only use a gas heater if your greenhouse has an in-built vent or chimney.

Kerosene Heaters

Kerosene heaters are generally not recommended, firstly, because they pose a significant fire risk. Secondly, they release plenty of air pollutants, including carbon monoxide, sulfur dioxide, nitrogen oxides, polycyclic aromatic hydrocarbons, and phthalates. This means that you can only operate a kerosene or paraffin heater in a well-ventilated area which defeats the purpose of using it in a greenhouse where you want to keep the warm air trapped for as long as possible. You simply light a wick on the paraffin heater, and it draws liquid fuel from a holding vessel. These heaters usually include a safety feature that extinguishes the flame immediately if it falls; nonetheless, you can never be too careful or too comfortable around an open flame.

Wood Stove

A wood stove is a sustainable method for heating your greenhouse. Although sustainable, you will need to add more wood throughout the night in the winter.

This is not practical at a time when you can simply purchase a myriad of other less labor-intensive heaters. Firewood heaters also require that your chimney be adequately insulated at the point where it passes through your greenhouse. Thus, you will be spending a lot of money and effort on your greenhouse for a labor-intensive process that keeps you up all night.

Finally, there is the more advantageous rocket mass heater. Rocket mass heaters are very efficient because they are deliberately and intricately built into the greenhouse. It works by channeling combustion gases through the greenhouse when the wood is burned. This way, the escaping combustion gases heat the greenhouse as they are escaping the combustion chamber.

Unheated Greenhouse/Heating Your Greenhouse for Free

The idea of an unheated greenhouse is not as absurd as it sounds. It is an easy method for heating your greenhouse without the labor-intensive work usually associated with other forms of heating. An unheated greenhouse can be used to grow more hardy vegetables in colder months. It will also enable you to start the more tender annuals and propagate perennials.

In extreme cold, you can add one or two layers of horticultural fleece over your plants at night to keep them toasty and warm. Remember that if you are cold, your plants are cold, so give them the same amount of love and care as you would give yourself in the winter. You can also layer the inside of your greenhouse with horticultural bubble wrap to keep your plants warm during the night; the sunlight can still penetrate the bubble wrap. Use the bubble wrap to swaddle your pots to insulate the roots of your plants, simultaneously preventing any clay pots from cracking.

You may grow your greens (lettuce, spinach, etc.) and other cold-tolerant vegetables, like broccoli, Brussels sprouts, peas, celery, or root vegetables, like carrots, beetroots, sweet potatoes, and parsnips, during this period. It is wholly recommended because winter temperatures stimulate sugar production in many root vegetables. Perennial herbs, such as fennel, chives, parsley, and oregano, do well in this environment, as do cool-hardy flowers, such as pansies, chrysanthemums, and calendulas.

VENTILATION

Your greenhouse can get too hot when direct sunlight enters the south and west-facing walls. In this case, your plants will literally cook. All greenhouses also come with vents for this reason. When your greenhouse rises above a comfortable temperature for your plants—usually 80-85 degrees Fahrenheit—then you can open the vents to allow hot air to escape through the top. Cool air, conversely, rests at the bottom, so you can open the door to allow cool air to escape. If the sun is very bright, it can still overheat your greenhouse in the colder months, so always keep an eye on your plants and do not make the mistake of believing that your greenhouse cannot overheat in the winter.

Opening and closing the vents manually is cheaper, but it comes with a downside. Should you forget to open or close your vents and doors at the appropriate time, you could damage or kill your plants. If you open the door, prop it with a heavy object to prevent it from closing without your knowledge, trapping your plants in extreme heat. You run the same risk if you are not often home in time to operate the ventilation manually. Conclusively, you will need to be close by for each sudden change in the weather. This is not feasible, so most people choose an automatic ventilation system.

The automatic ventilation system has a sensor that automatically turns on the fan(s) and a heating system every time the temperature inside the greenhouse becomes too hot or too cold. It is, essentially, a greenhouse thermostat. You should invest in additional stand fans to allow for maximum ventilation for your plants.

AUTOMATIC VENT OPENERS

Automatic vent openers automatically control the temperature and humidity levels in your greenhouse. That is, they provide additional ventilation when it gets too hot or humid in your greenhouse. Since they are automatic, it relieves you of the unending task of regularly checking if your vents need to be opened or closed, making gardening more accessible. It also reduces the worry and anxiety if you are away and unable to check your vents for a considerable period.

By design, the air inside your greenhouse will always warm up following temperature rises. As a countermeasure, your automatic vent will gradually open to allow the correct amount of airflow into your greenhouse. Once your greenhouse cools and the temperature drops, the vent will automatically close to prevent your plants from becoming too cold.

Vent openers are heat-activated. A metal cylinder that contains a waxy mineral expands when heated, pushing a piston that opens your vent. As the air cools, the mineral shrinks and a spring closes the vent—resetting the piston. Because the vent gradually opens and closes, it allows just the right amount of airflow for cooling and heating. This means your plants are constantly receiving the ideal amount of heat for perfect growing conditions. The automatic vent opener is an easy-install, easy-use, efficient, and pivotal tool for your greenhouse.

You can also purchase circulation fans for your greenhouse. They provide incredible airflow, distributing CO2 around the greenhouse evenly to promote healthy plant growth. They distribute both fresh air and heated air around your greenhouse whenever required due to temperature changes. Unlike the automatic vent opener, the circulation fan is electric but is automated with a thermostat that turns it on and off when temperatures drop or increase. Using both the vent opener and fans together makes circulation within your greenhouse more efficient. The automatic vent opener controls temperature, while the fan eliminates cold and hot spots congregated in your greenhouse.

If you have a medium or large greenhouse, you can consider using an evaporative air cooler, also called a pad or swamp cooler. These are the most effective cooling systems for a greenhouse if you don't want to use an air conditioner. It pumps water over special cooling pads, lowering the temperature of the hot greenhouse air passing through them; a blower then pushes the cooled air back into the greenhouse. It works in conjunction with your automatic roof vent, which exhausts hot air from the greenhouse. Like circulation fans, they are also automated using electric thermostats.

One further benefit of the evaporative air cooler is that its cooling pads act as filters to keep insects, dust, and pollen out. It essentially keeps your greenhouse's air clean and breathable for your plants.

SHADE

You can use a shade cloth to adequately shade your greenhouse. Shade cloths come in green or any other dark-colored material. They are typically made out of polyethylene and polypropylene and come in different densities and degrees of shade—these densities of shade range from 5 percent to 95 percent.

The percentage of the shade cloth signifies the amount of light that is blocked by the fabric. You must choose the proper density because this will allow enough sunlight to penetrate the greenhouse, allowing for healthy growth. For example, with an 80 percent shade cloth, you can produce healthy cabbages, lettuces, peppers, and irises. With a 75 percent shade cloth, you can grow large olive trees and orchids.

They work by rolling down like a window shade over the outside of your greenhouse windows. You can roll the shade cloth up or down—according to weather and climatic conditions. Doing this, you adjust the temperature and light levels inside the greenhouse.

Shade cloth also protects your plants from the radiant energy captured from the sun in the daytime. Radiant energy quickly builds up, increasing the temperature in your greenhouse to levels that are dangerous for your plants.

During active photosynthesis, your plants need blue to red range lights within the 400-700 nanometers range on the light spectrum. Anything higher or lower will damage your plants. Similarly, excessive amounts of infrared light—especially in the far end of the spectrum—can lead to discoloration, early bloom, early growth spurts, and even death.

Given that plants only need only 1.5-2% of transmitted sunlight for photosynthesis, shade cloth reflects or partially blocks out most of these rays. Shade cloths also reduce light levels in your greenhouse by 75%—acting as a solar collector and turning it into heat. In the evaporative cooling process, the temperature of your shade cloth increases to higher than the temperature of the air in the greenhouse. Heat energy goes up into the air while cool energy falls—cooling the plants placed at the bottom of the greenhouse.

There are two types of shade clothe: woven and knitted. Woven shade cloth is typically 30% heavier, more expensive and more challenging to install. Most shade cloths are water-resistant.

The best shade cloth for a greenhouse is water-resistant knitted because of its durability and versatility. Most vegetables prefer a 30-50% shade cloth, while plants prefer a 30-60% shade cloth. Hence, you can grow both side-by-side.

You must measure the width and lengths of the roof of your greenhouse before buying a shade cloth, as when installed, it should drape down the sides from the roof. The best is to measure the distance from the top of the roof to two-thirds down the sides of your greenhouse. Remember that you don't need to cover the sides of your greenhouse entirely because you still need sunlight to enter.

To install the shade cloth, you must:

1. Attach S-hooks to the base of your greenhouse, 2 feet apart. It needs to be 2 feet apart because the cloth grommets on your shade cloth are also 2 feet apart.
2. Carefully place the shade cloth over the roof of the greenhouse.
3. Use bungee cords to attach the grommets to the hooks in the base.
4. Use snap-on clamps to secure the cloth onto your PVC pipe greenhouse.

5. Use lock channels to secure the cloth onto your aluminum or wood greenhouse.

HUMIDITY

Did You Know?

Since the 1900s, some 75 percent of plant genetic diversity has been lost as farmers worldwide have left their multiple local varieties and landraces for genetically uniform, high-yielding varieties.

If you are growing tropical plants in your greenhouse, you must be pretty excited to watch them germinate. Mangoes, papayas, oranges, coconuts, and many more beautiful fruits enrich and flavor our lives. For your tropical plants to thrive, you must make your greenhouse as humid as possible since humidity is what tropical plants crave.

It is in your plants' best interest to control the humidification and dehumidification inside your greenhouse. While humidity is an essential factor for keeping your plants alive, many greenhouse plants are susceptible to fungal infections. Although some plants, such as tropical plants, love a highly humid greenhouse, your succulents could be at risk for fungal infections. For this reason, you need to balance the humidity within your greenhouse attentively.

During daylight, plant transpiration releases vapor which becomes trapped in the greenhouse. At night, when the temperature drops and your greenhouse glazing gets cold, the temperature inside your greenhouse drops, causing this vapor to turn into condensation (when water vapor changes to liquid). At this point, you will need to reduce the liquid in the greenhouse to prevent plants from developing mildew, rot, or botrytis blight.

Air circulation will keep the humidity in your greenhouse just right. If ambient moisture (moisture on the surface of your crops) is too high, you can use a ventilator to exchange the moist interior air with cool, dry exterior air. Using ventilators is energy-intensive and not as effective as other methods. You will also need to heat the air coming into the greenhouse to keep it from becoming too cold. Naturally, heating the air uses a lot of energy and has a financial impact.

Another method for dehumidifying the air in your greenhouse is condensation. Contemporary greenhouses use multiple wall glazing, screens, and curtains, which have the disadvantage of trapping humidity inside your greenhouse at a greater rate. This creates a warmer greenhouse interior and makes it more challenging to control the humidity. With condensation, the air inside your greenhouse is drawn across a cold refrigerant coil while water condenses and drains away. Unfortunately, the drawn-in air traps in soil dust, fertilizer, warm air, and plant debris—creating the conditions for bacteria and mold to grow inside the condenser, which is then released back into your greenhouse. In which case, you prevent your plants from fungal infections by infecting them with bacteria.

The good news for us is there's a more efficient method known as a synergistic liquid desiccant dehumidification system. Desiccant dehumidification uses a desiccant material, like salt, to absorb moisture or water vapor from the air. This process is highly efficient because it keeps the humidity level in the air at your desired level. Desiccant dehumidification reduces the annual energy consumption needed for heating your greenhouse by about 60%, compared with ventilation.

This dehumidification system, created in 1955, works by using the dehumidifier to dehumidify hot and humid air from the ambient condition in the greenhouse (Chen et al., 2020). The air conditioning system then cools the hot and humid air (e.g., cooling water, evaporative cooling system, vapor compression system, and so on.). A strong liquid desiccant solution absorbs moisture from the ambient air in the dehumidifier, thereby becoming a weak, diluted solution. This weak solution is then passed through the regenerator to be re-concentrated.

One significant advantage of this system is that it removes indoor air pollutants and improves air quality. An additional benefit is that desiccant materials can absorb inorganic and organic contaminants during the dehumidification process. This means that the absorption process can remove biological pollutants, such as bacteria, fungi, and viruses, significantly improving indoor air quality and reducing your risk of bacterial, fungal, and viral infections. In addition, it provides a controlled temperature and humidity for food production, maintaining optimal conditions for happy, thriving plants in your greenhouse.

Conversely, the simplest way to reduce greenhouse humidity is to use a fan or blower connected to a humidistat, both working in conjunction with a heater to maintain consistent temperatures. Another simplistic method is to avoid any standing water in the greenhouse as this forms droplets that lead to humidity. Use drip irrigation to apply water directly to plant roots, thus preventing ambient moisture from forming. Drip irrigation has the added benefit of preventing the leaves from staying wet, risking ripe conditions for fungal pathogens to breed.

Using wood chips and pebbles is a simple method to keep your plants from becoming too dry. You may use the methods above to keep your greenhouse dehumidified and use the methods below to keep your plants' roots well-watered.

Pebbles

- Place trays of pebbles underneath your plants. Fill the tray with a single layer of pebbles and add enough water until it reaches just about halfway up the pebbles. As the water evaporates, this will create a naturally humid environment for your plants. Keep adding water as the level drops.
- Alternatively, put marbles or stone chips on the floor under the plant benches or tables. These can also help create humidity if they're dampened down on a dry day.

Wood Chips

- Wood chips work just like marbles. Simply place marbles or wood chips under the tables of your plants. On dry days, dampen them to add more humidity to your plants' roots.

- One of the most vital conditions for your plants' well-being is the weather. Plants need good weather conditions to survive.
- Plant survival is dependent on air, water, soil, and sunlight. If their surroundings are too hot or too cold, then your plants will die or barely grow.
- Four variables control the weather conditions within your greenhouse. They are heating, ventilation, shade, and humidity.

In the next chapter, you will learn the fundamental tools needed to start a greenhouse.

CHAPTER FIVE

Greenhouse Materials and Equipment

"The first supermarket supposedly appeared on the American landscape in 1946. That is not very long ago. Until then, where was all the food? Dear folks, the food was in homes, gardens, local fields, and forests. It was near kitchens, near tables, near bedsides. It was in the pantry, the cellar, the backyard."

—Joel Salatin

The best greenhouse materials and equipment are pivotal for managing a greenhouse efficiently. The type of equipment and materials you use will depend on the type of greenhouse you own. For example, if you have a small greenhouse, you might not need complicated irrigation or ventilation equipment. If you have a giant greenhouse, you will require a more extensive range of equipment and will also have the space to store larger equipment. On the other hand, if you have a small greenhouse, your requirements are more minor, like soil sample testing kits, trowels, or watering cans.

Your greenhouse equipment will help you with the following:

- Lighting
- Water management—Irrigation and drainage, sink, or hose access
- Ventilation
- Climate control (cooling and heating)
- Pest control

The equipment and materials you purchase will last a long time, so think of them as an investment in your perfect greenhouse. No matter the size or type of greenhouse that you own, you will need specific essential equipment. These are:

- Planters, pots, trays.
- Potting soil.
- Watering can.
- Wheelbarrow
- Sanitizers.
- Seed starters.
- Moisture meter.
- Light meter.
- Thermometer.
- pH and soil test kits
- Greenhouse furniture.

BENCHES

You must choose a suitable bench that keeps your plants healthy and thriving. You can either choose a rolling or stationary bench. A rolling bench provides efficient greenhouse space by allowing you to move it and optimize your grow space for optimal crop yield by eliminating walkways.

Stationary benches are usually wooden and less expensive than the typical metal rolling benches. Despite this, wooden benches can be more costly in the long term because they require more maintenance, are more difficult to disinfect and degrade faster. Even if you choose a stationary metal bench, it does not come with the flexibility offered by a rolling bench, and you would lose valuable crop space that a rolling bench would afford you.

Besides the stationary or rolling classifications, there are three major types of benches to choose from to complete your greenhouse. They are:

Flood Benches

Also known as flood and drain systems, ebb and flow benches, or sub-irrigation systems, flood benches allow water to travel upwards to the roots through capillary action. They are inspired by nature, where plants draw their water from the ground below.

Benefits

- Conserves water, with up to 90% less water usage.
- Conserves greenhouse material, including up to 90% less fertilizer usage and significantly fewer chemicals (particularly fungicides)
- You don't need to stand around watering individual pots or regularly worry about the watering needs of each plant.
- Promotes even plant growth since all plants are watered simultaneously and evenly.

- More efficient—proven to reduce your crop growth cycle by one to two weeks.
- Keeps your bench area free of hoses and watering cans.
- Dry floors—make it easier to control the humidity in your warehouse.
- Lowers plant disease—because your plants' leaves remain dry.

The flood bench re-circulates any unused water and fertilizer. Principally, it recycles what the plants don't use for the next watering or fertilizing cycle. From the benefits list above, you can tell that choosing a flood bench is environmentally friendly.

Expanded Metal Tops

Expanded metal tops, also known as metal greenhouse benches, are more economical and offer better flexibility for greenhouses with many crop varieties. Since they complete water drainage and air circulation through their open diamond design, expanded metal tops help prevent mold and fungus growth. They are also resistant to corrosion and rust.

Trough Benches

Like flood benches, trough benches are great for bottom watering your pots. The aluminum troughs are flat on the bottom with short sides.

The trough is placed on supports, pitched slightly from the inlet to the outlet, aiding water flow using gravity. If you choose, you can leave an air gap between adjacent troughs, but this is unnecessary. A significant disadvantage of the trough bench is its shallow irrigation head, which calls for relatively long contact times if you want thorough irrigation. However, the volume of nutrient solution that you would need to use is smaller if you choose troughs because the water head is shallower and the flooded area is smaller. You can line your trough with a capillary mat to reduce the chances of water channeling in the shallow flow.

Similarly, troughs boast a greater gap between each irrigation trough because there is reduced flexibility for adjusting pot sizes. This is good news for your plants because they will dry more evenly with more space between them. It also enables you to re-circulate water, cutting down on your fertilizer consumption.

SANITIZERS

You will need to sanitize your greenhouse regularly. You will recognize cleaning time for your greenhouse when you suffer recurring problems with diseases such as *Pythium* root rot or with an influx of insects. In a greenhouse, infectious microbes multiply quickly. At the same time, algae flourish on moist surfaces, creating the perfect conditions for fungus gnats and shore flies to thrive.

You must disinfect between crop cycles when your greenhouse is empty. Cleaning as early as possible is recommended because it helps you to eliminate overwintering sites and, in turn, prevents pests from reducing their populations before the spring growing season; prevention is better than cure. After thoroughly cleaning your entire greenhouse, you should use a sanitizer containing hydrogen peroxide and peroxyacetic acid (SaniDate) to flush out slime and debris. Sanitizers will curb the number of pathogens and algae, most of which can attack your plants and some of which can attack you.

Algae are a diverse plant group that likes to grow in wet, moist, and damp environments, including walks, water pipes, gardening equipment, greenhouse coverings, and inside plant pots. Algae is a major problem for your greenhouse because it creates an impermeable layer on surfaces that hinders the watering process. It clogs irrigation, misting lines and emitters, acts as a food source for insect pests and increases the danger of slippery surfaces. Water supplies are the perfect medium for algae to move into your greenhouse, and the conditions inside are ideal for the algae to survive, as it is warm, moist, and bursting with fertilizer.

To avoid algae, practice safe and proper water management and fertilization. This practice will slow down the algae rate of growth. Don't over-water or slow-grow your plants, particularly during the early stages of the production cycle. Always allow the surface of the irrigation bench to dry out between watering. This is imperative since irrigation water can also carry and transmit pathogens.

IRRIGATION

The last chapter covered how to implement a drainage system in your greenhouse. Irrigating your plants simply means watering your plants using a specific method of watering. There are three critical rules for irrigating your plants. They are:

- Precise watering.
  - The precise amount of water is vital for your plants' survival. Under-watering and over-watering will cause your plant to suffer. Always check that the root substrates are aerated and emptied as this will prevent over-watering or under-watering, giving your plants a better chance of thriving.
- Thorough watering.
  - Water your plants' roots thoroughly each time to refresh your plant adequately.
- Healthy watering.
  - Do not wait until your plants are too dry before watering them, as this can cause them to go into moisture stress. Healthy watering leads to healthy roots and a healthy plant.

There are several methods of irrigating your greenhouse, and they include:

- Hand Watering
- Overhead Sprinkler
- Boom Watering
- Drip Irrigation
- Tube Watering
- Ebb and Flow Watering
- Perimeter Watering

The most tried and tested irrigation system, hand watering, is a traditional agriculture and horticulture method because of its cumbersome qualities. If you have a small greenhouse, then hand watering remains economical. It is also economical when watering seedbeds, selected pots, or areas that have dried sooner than others. Otherwise, you are better off using a more economical irrigation method.

Overhead Sprinkler

If you are growing crops, you should keep the foliage dry at all times for disease control purposes. However, if you are growing bedding plants or green plants, you can water from overhead because it is economical. It is straightforward to set up, and water distribution will always be uniform.

Fertigation System

In the irrigation and fertilization process, fertigation is a system where plants are fertilized and irrigated simultaneously, using fertilized solutions. Since it combines two necessary greenhouse processes, the system saves time, labor, and money. Even better, the system is consistent, ensuring that plants get the same amount of fertilizer every time. This encourages uniformity of plant growth and improves nutrient uptake because fertilizer and water are applied to the roots. As a result, plants develop a healthier root system, helping to save water and to minimize nutrient losses.

You must constantly monitor all components within the fertigation system as faults will lead to uneven nutrient distribution. It may also lead to overfertilization or leaching of nutrients when excess water is applied to crops. The water tank can also become clogged, given that the fertilizer can react with calcium and magnesium bicarbonates in the water. You need corrosion-resistant equipment to build a fertigation system. Likewise, you can only use readily soluble or liquid fertilizers.

Ebb and Flow Irrigation System

The ebb and flow irrigation system is generally daunting for beginner greenhouse gardeners. Also known as the flood and drain irrigation system, this method is the most popular hydroponic system used in greenhouses. When using this system, you can grow flats in level, nutrient-rich water inside a tray. As the name suggests, any unused water is drained back into the reservoir using gravity. It is inexpensive to set up, although initially expensive to purchase components. Like many hydroponic methods, it is also very versatile.

Even if you are a beginner, you can still choose the ebb and flow system because it is easy to assemble and easy to use. It might be daunting to see the number of components that need to be assembled, but don't let this put you off. Unfortunately, using the flood and drain system results in high relative humidity that can build up in the greenhouse—building up condensation. In return, condensation can lead to foliar diseases.

Boom Watering

Boom watering is used when seedlings are growing in plug trays. It typically consists of a water pipe boom extended from one side of your greenhouse bay to another. The boom is fitted with nozzles that spray either water or fertilizer solution onto the crop. While this is an affordable irrigation system, it can contribute to soil infertility while it causes waterlogging and depletion of water sources. Water-borne diseases can be spread by the boom watering system.

Perimeter Watering System

Perimeter watering uses a plastic pipe around the perimeter of a bench or bed with nozzles that spray water onto the soil below the foliage. The plastic pipe can either be PVC or polythene, with nozzles attached, allowing water distribution below the foliage.

The perimeter watering system is best used when growing flowers.

Drip Irrigation (Tube Watering)

Also known as trickle irrigation, drip irrigation is set up by attaching small plastic tubes beside or beneath your plants. Water then "drips" into the soil at regular intervals through small, watering and fertilizing your plants uniformly. Drip irrigation offers about 90% efficiency, compared to 60-80% of other irrigation types. Although, this is dependent upon soil type, level of the field, and how water is applied to the furrows.

Another advantage is its provision of maximum control over environmental variability. It provides excellent production with very little water use while conserving soil and fertilizer nutrients and cutting costs.

Drip or trickle irrigation is, essentially, the best means of water conservation. When calculated for its use over a long period, the equipment to set up drip irrigation is relatively inexpensive, but its one-off cost can be prohibitive. You may want to juggle its efficiency with its inefficiency since the risk of degrading plastic affects the soil content—thereby placing your plants at considerable risk.

Also known as drip irrigation or trickle irrigation, tube watering irrigation is commonly used to water plant pots using a polyethylene microtube. These microtubes come in different sizes, with different inner diameters placed in a line around your plants. As a cost-effective irrigation system, the tubes apply low water flow directly to the soil, keeping the plants from being overwhelmed with watering. Instead, it gently applies water to the root system consistently. You will need to weigh down the microtubes so that the plants are watered at regular speed intervals.

PROPAGATORS

A propagator is a compact incubator used for raising seedlings in a controlled, optimum environment. It has an undertray, filled with soil or another growing medium, and a transparent cover. More or less, it is a miniature greenhouse that lets the light in and retains moisture and heat. They come in various shapes and styles but are not manufactured with built-in thermostats and heating.

Propagators often have ventilation slots that allow fresh air in and condensation out on hotter days. Many greenhouse enthusiasts require propagators during early spring because nighttime temperatures are often too low for germination.

Propagators are a greenhouse necessity. They allow the gardener to grow strong, young plants—healthy and ready to plant once the weather warms up. You will use them while your plants are still very young and vulnerable to offer protection from pests, cold, and other outside influences until they are strong enough to grow outside on their own. Like earlier advice to build a more extensive greenhouse than you think you need, it is more fiscal to purchase a larger propagator than you may need. Think about how many pots and trays you will be able to fit into the propagator and make sure that the one you choose has enough space—and then more.

A heat mat (also called a propagation mat) keeps your baby plants even warmer during the cold. It is highly recommended because the air temperature is usually warmer than the soil temperature. They keep your seeds happy, causing them to germinate quickly and with ease.

THERMOMETER

You cannot run a greenhouse without a thermometer as you need to monitor the temperature at all times; your plants depend on a constant optimum temperature for survival. Plants are vulnerable and sensitive to temperature changes which can cause them to become deformed or die. Your plants are susceptible to overheating in summer and to frost during the winter. The ideal temperature for your greenhouse is determined by the types of plants you cultivate.

Furthermore, you will need two types of thermometers. The first is a digital thermometer to monitor the temperature; the second is a hygrometer. The hygrometer determines the amount of water vapor in the air. This is important to check consistently because some plants will need a more or less humid environment to thrive.

A wireless digital thermometer is best to check and monitor temperatures in your greenhouse. You can use a traditional analog thermometer, but the digital thermometer is more efficient. Standard equipment can be used for your greenhouse gardening needs, but relying on more advanced tools can make all the difference. For example, using an automatic vent opener is more efficient and less time-consuming than opening and closing vents by hand. Identically, a digital greenhouse thermometer is designed to record a specific timeframe's minimum and maximum temperature (usually 24 hours). This way, you can build a longitudinal timeframe of the temperature within your greenhouse, helping you decipher what the temperature inside your greenhouse should be based on the climate, the season, the days' weather, and the thermometer's average recorded temperatures.

There's a vast difference between a sunny day and a chilly summer night, depending on your climate, and insight into these fluctuations is essential. Although the digital thermometer is more expensive than the analog, it usually doubles as a hygrometer, saving you the expense of purchasing two costly measuring devices. A thermometer-hygrometer digitally displays the current temperature and humidity for easy viewing, ensuring that you have the proper humidity and temperature conditions to grow your plants.

SHELVES

Shelves are generally attached to the interior of your greenhouse walls. Shelves are critical—even for small greenhouses as they keep your structure spacious and straightforward. The mental health benefits diminish when your greenhouse is cluttered, untidy, and lacks space. As a result, if you are constantly in an untidy greenhouse, your thoughts and emotions might feel chaotic and unorganized. There is also the increased likelihood of tripping or falling on objects left haphazardly on the floor or surfaces around the greenhouse, so it is wise to use shelves to make the best use of your available space. It also provides you storage space for your greenhouse materials and equipment, for example, your seeds, pots, and gardening gloves. If you want versatility, use a bench instead of a built-in shelf. With a moveable bench, you can create more space to make room for more plants and rearrange the greenhouse as needed.

You will need at least one dedicated potting shelf or bench. Ensure that it is smooth and heavy-duty so that it can hold your equipment without falls or breakages. The potting shelf should be at waist height to avoid bending over repeatedly. You will use it to prepare your seed flats and transplant them; keeping them separate prevents you from regularly disturbing your other plants.

If you plant flowers, you will need aluminum shelves for your flowerpots. Flowers need more sunlight and will die if placed on the ground. Keep your flower pots on the top shelf, ensuring that they do not take up unnecessary space on the ground. Install your aluminum shelf on the side of the greenhouse that gets the most sunlight to promote happy growth for your flowers.

A greenhouse is a very structured environment, and as you embark on this journey, you may need to employ the service of an engineer to work out mathematical measurements for you. While greenhouse gardening is a creative and philosophical endeavor, it is also a mathematical and mechanical one. Structured thinking will help you organize your greenhouse in the most efficient way possible.

Like all things, organizing your greenhouse creates order and structure. It is best to divide it into sections as it is no fun spending 20 minutes searching for your left glove, seeds, or even a specific plant. Instead, meticulously plan where everything should be, factoring in the best position of each item and piece of equipment in relation to its use. This means that the aluminum shelf should be on the side that receives the most light, and your seeds will be far from the irrigation system because they will begin to germinate if they get wet. What is the best position for your ventilation cooler or fan in the greenhouse? And how do you safely store your soil without damage? These are all essential questions that can quickly be answered by creating a drawing with labels of where everything goes inside the greenhouse will assist you in your organization. Think about the different sections and what you will place on each shelf or bench, and the optimal place for such an item? Figuring out the best use of your space means that you can plan and implement the structure within your greenhouse once without a need for constant changes.

Measure your greenhouse to avoid purchasing and having to return items that do not fit. You can avoid wasting time, labor, effort, and money by measuring everything twice and purchasing good-quality products in the correct sizes. High-quality products last much longer so, while they may be expensive at the time of purchase, they are the more economical option in the long term.

If you have a greenhouse with a transparent covering, you need to be aware of shadows created by shelves and pieces of equipment. If your plants are on the lower shelf, shadows will reduce the amount of light they receive, hindering their growth. If this is the case, you will have to raise your plants to a level not touched by shadows. If your greenhouse uses a translucent covering that provides diffused light, you won't have any issues with shadows and can place your plants on the ground if necessary.

CHAPTER SUMMARY

- The best greenhouse materials and equipment are pivotal for managing a greenhouse efficiently.
- While the sun may heat your greenhouse naturally, you would still need a heating system to ensure a constant temperature all year round.
- The type of equipment and materials you use will depend on the type of greenhouse you own.
- No matter the size or type of greenhouse that you own, you will need specific essential equipment.
- You will need to sanitize your greenhouse regularly. You will know it is time to clean your greenhouse when you suffer recurring problems with diseases.
- To avoid algae, practice safe and proper water management and fertilization.
- Propagators and automatic vent openers are a greenhouse necessity.

In the next chapter, you will learn:

- The types of seeds greenhouse gardeners can use in their environments.
- How to create the perfect environment to grow different types of seeds.
- The advantages of hybrid seeds.
- Understanding the seed labels.

CHAPTER SIX

Seeds

"Gardening is an assertion of influence on a small piece of the environment—that's influence, not control. A wise gardener seeks to channel the elements of the garden's environment—soil, plants, critters, weather—to produce a small community of beauty and abundance. Trying too hard to rigidly control the garden generally leads to results that are sterile—literally and figuratively—and dull.
Achieving the effect you want with the right mix of effort and letting things take their own course is tremendously satisfying. A wall covered with rich purple clematis, or a flower bed that gradually rises from sprawling blue geranium to towering yellow cup plants, makes me feel that the world can be handled to create beautiful results."

—Jason Kay

Seeds are at the heart of your greenhouse. In fact, seeds are at the heart of life on our planet. Without seeds, there is no life on Earth. Concurrently, without seeds, there is no life in your greenhouse.

Once you have planned and executed your greenhouse's technicalities, you now have time to seriously consider what you want to plant. You may have already decided on the exact plants you would like to cultivate. Alternatively, you may have a general idea of what you would like to grow, with no specific list of plants. This is the part of the process that requires creativity. As a gardener, your hands give birth to earthly beauty. Perhaps you want plants that bring texture, geometry, and color to your greenhouse. Maybe you want to grow plants with incredible scents to welcome aromatherapy into your life. It might be the case that you desire to plant food crops, eager to feed yourself and your loved ones with good, healthy, non-toxic food.

Understanding how seeds work will enable you to formulate the perfect growing plan at whatever stage of the planning process. When you understand seeds, you can engage with them competently.

THE RULES

When it comes to greenhouses, you have the perfect environment to grow any different types of seeds. To make sure you stay organized with your seed storages, follow these simple rules:

- Keep everything labeled.
- Be smart.
- Check the germination rate on the seeds.
- The seed packs should tell you if the seeds will provide you with more seedlings.
- Invest in containers for your seeds.

SAVING YOUR SEEDS

You will need to collect seeds from your plants for your greenhouse. Buying seeds every year is not economical and defeats the primary purpose of a greenhouse: Becoming self-sufficient and independently producing your crops is a better way.

Collecting seeds is generally straightforward. Some plants like most herbs, beans, peas, radishes, and lettuce, are annuals, and others, like carrots, parsnips, chards, beets, parsley, onions, and leeks, are biennials. Annuals are plants that produce seeds in the same year as they grow. Biennials produce seeds in the second year when they grow a seed stalk. Sometimes biennials bolt, meaning that they throw up seed stalks even in the same year that they grow. Seed saving is one of the ways to propagate your plants.

Mother Nature evolved to find alternative ways to grow, protect and propagate plant species by various methods. This is a failsafe imperative. If one propagation method fails or is threatened, another propagation means will give a plant species another chance of survival.

Like french tarragon and lavender, some plants make reproduction problematic because their seeds are tough to start and often sterile. Plants, like garlic, are fertile and produce seed stalk; however, it takes years for the seeds to grow, reach maturation and harvest. These plants are better propagated by live cuttings. Garlic, for example, is grown when its root bulb is divided and used as a seed. Other vegetables and fruits such as peas, beans, and corn kernels are actually seeds, so you can replant these.

To save your seeds, you must select samples from the healthiest and most vigorous plants. These are easy to identify, as they are usually the first plants to germinate. Follow Mother Nature's cue and select a comprehensive sample from various parts of the growing area. This way, you have spares in case one sample does not propagate successfully. To save seeds, simply pick them from overripe fruit, place them in a mesh strainer, rinse very well and dry on a paper towel.

Do not plant varieties within a species (plant families) too close together in your greenhouse. Species like cucumbers, melons, zucchinis, and squashes will interbreed if grown too close together. Separating plant families prevents interbreeding and reduces the likelihood of growing hybrid vegetables that won't taste right.

HYBRID SEEDS

Hybrid seeds are available at almost any garden store. They produce more and can be harvested earlier, and can grow larger than most greenhouse plants. They may be more expensive but are more durable.

Hybrid seeds are genetically more robust because they combine two different varieties of the same plant. These are known as F1 hybrid seeds, so-called because they result from breeding two different strains to produce a new variety. F1 stands for, Filial 1, or "first children." To produce a good supply of these F1 seeds, a breeder must maintain two pure, true varieties of each parent variety and keep a good stock of breeding plants that are usually hand pollinated. The breeder has to cross-pollinate varieties repeatedly, recording the results, until a hybrid formula emerges that produces consistently excellent results. Excellent results depend on the breeder's aim. Perhaps aspiring to breed an orange plant with more juicy oranges that retain their flavor, a dedication process that can take many years. The objective is to breed the best genetic traits of both parent plants and combine them into a more vigorous hybrid seed.

The dedication required and time taken to create hybrid seeds is what causes them to be more expensive, in contrast to their non-hybrid, open-pollinated (OP) varieties.

In hand pollination, the breeder extracts pollen from the male flower of one plant and transfers it to the female flower of a different plant. Once pollination is successful, the ovary of the female flower begins to swell and form fruit. Inside this fruit, F1 hybrid seeds develop.

Hybrid seeds are more attractive for farmers and horticulturists because they produce "super" plants and crops. The results could mean sweeter mangoes, more disease-resistant roses, more produce in the vineyard, or earlier maturity for tomato crops. The possibilities are numerous. Frequently, hybrid seeds become heirloom seeds because they are so well-received by the public that agriculturalists use them repeatedly, saving them throughout a generation before passing them to the next.

The disadvantage of storing a hybrid seed for future use is its genetic unpredictability. The seed carries traits from both mother and father plants; you cannot choose or control which traits from which parent be dominant when you plant your seed. If you plan to save the seeds from your plants, it might be safer to save the more predictable open-pollinated seed varieties. Furthermore, hybrid seeds are held back by what is known as "hybrid vigor." The primary benefit of a first-generation hybrid seed, which agriculturists love, is that it grows very well. Unfortunately, the second generation seeds (F2) lose all their hybrid vigor, often resulting in unremarkable plants. This drives up the price of hybrid seeds because breeders recognize that the buyer cannot keep the offspring of his first-generation seed for the following year.

For you, the amateur botanist, this means that you must plan your budget accordingly. Can you afford to purchase hybrid seeds every year? Are the benefits worth it to you, and do they perfectly meet your needs? Planting ten varieties of OP fruit and vegetables that will sustain you throughout the year might be better than planting just two hybrid crops that, admittedly, might taste great but won't sustain you at all. Indeed, if your goal is to save your seeds each year for economic and agricultural sustenance, then using hybrid seeds is not ideal. Seed saving is also environmentally friendly. It improves biodiversity and eliminates using excessive water, fertilizer, and heat to develop a one-time seed. As a gardener, protecting the environment is very likely a passion of yours. In this case, hybrid seeds might not be for you.

HEIRLOOM SEEDS

Heirloom seeds are the most popular seeds gardeners use when starting. They are easy to store and last a long time before planting. They also provide great vegetables and flavors. It is better to buy them from your local market because these seeds will be used in the local environment by nature of their history.

Heirloom seeds are also known as heritage seeds and open-pollinated seeds. They are very old seeds that produce great tasting, smelling, and looking plants. To be genuinely classified as an heirloom, the seeds must have a documented heritage passed down from generation to generation within a family or a local community. An heirloom plant (whether vegetable, fruit, or flower) must "breed true." That means they must be open-pollinated or naturally pollinated (by insects, birds, wind, or other natural means). They must also retain their original traits from one generation to the next.

An additional advantage of the heirloom seed is its quasi-organic status. A significant proportion of heirloom seeds are organic. You can source heirloom seeds from local families or local farms. If this is not possible in the area where you live, specialized catalogs and online stores sell heirloom seeds to amateur and avid gardeners. One such catalog is Seed Savers Exchange (https://www.seedsavers.org/), which helped pioneer the heirloom seed movement and continues its work today to preserve, circulate, and sell rare and heirloom seeds in the U.S.

There is a wide selection of heirloom seeds in the U.S, but for the greenhouse on a budget, these are relatively expensive—especially if you want to use them as the primary source of your seeds. Your best alternative is to buy heirloom seeds for plants that prosper under the climatic conditions of your local area. Order plants that your family likes and crops that you and your family enjoy eating. Indeed, you can plan to share the costs of a seed package with another local or greenhouse gardener near you.

Fair warning! Once you taste the delicious, flavorful crops that heirloom seeds grow, you will not be able to return to store-bought vegetables or fruits. This is a common complaint of local, organic horticulturists whose palettes inevitably change for the better.

UNDERSTANDING SEED LABELS

According to the USDA (2007), the law requires that each seed lot offered for sale must be "truthfully labeled." Seed labels are regulated by the Federal Seed Act as well as state seed laws. In addition, all state certification agencies must comply with the minimum requirements and standards of the Association of Official Seed Certification Agencies (AOSCA). This ensures uniform testing methods and minimum standards of seed quality. The format of seed labels may be varied, but all labels will have some semblance of the following, as required by the Federal Seed Act.

- Origin: This is where the seed was grown.
- Variety and Kind: This is the cultivar/release name, species, and common name.
- Lot number: This is the series of letters or numbers assigned by the grower for tracking purposes.
- Net weight: This details the amount of material in the container.
- Percent inert matter: This is how much of the material in the bag is plant debris and materials other than seed.
- Percent pure seed (purity): This describes how much of the material is actually the seed.
- Percent other crop seeds: This is the percentage of other non-weed seeds.
- Percent weed seeds: This is the percentage of seeds considered weed species.
- Name of restricted noxious seed, including number per pound of seed: Noxious weed species vary state by state. There are two types of noxious

weeds: Restricted and prohibited. Restricted weeds are listed as seeds per pound of material in the bag. By law, there should be no prohibited weeds.

- Percent germination (germ): This describes how much of the seed will germinate readily.
- Hard seed: This explains which seed does not germinate readily because of a hard seed coat.
- Dormant seed: This is a seed that does not readily germinate because it requires that the soil be pre-treatment or weathered. (Some suppliers may combine hard and dormant seed on the label.)
- Germination test date: This is the date within 12 months of the planned date for using the seed.
- Name and address of the seller or grower responsible for analysis.

Key Phrases

The following key phrases will help you choose what seeds you need:

- Organic
  This word on the packet means that these seeds were grown organically according to rules and regulations. They are void of chemical substances.

- Non-GMO
  These seeds have not been tampered with using DNA technology.

- GMO
  These seeds were created from cross genes of different plants.

- Percent Germination
  This label will tell you what percentage of the seeds will sprout.

- Hard Seeds
  These seeds might need longer to grow because of the hard coat.

- Dormant Seeds
  These seeds don't sprout very easily and need some special treatment.

- Seeds are at the heart of your greenhouse.
- You will need to collect seeds from your plants for your greenhouse. Buying seeds every year is not economical and defeats the primary purpose of a greenhouse.
- Mother Nature evolved to find alternative ways to grow a plant, protect and propagate plant species by various methods.
- Do not plant varieties within a species (plant families) too close together in your greenhouse.
- Hybrid seeds are more attractive for farmers and horticulturists because they produce "super" plants and crops.
- Heirloom seeds are the most popular seeds gardeners use when starting. They are easy to store and last a long time before planting.

In the next chapter, you will learn the list of plants, fruits, and vegetables that can thrive ideally in a greenhouse environment and why they are good and good for you.

CHAPTER SEVEN
Flourishing My Greenhouse

"Anthropocentric as [the gardener] may be, he recognizes that he is dependent for his health and survival on many other forms of life, so he is careful to take their interests into account in whatever he does. He is, in fact, a wilderness advocate of a certain kind. It is when he respects and nurtures the wilderness of his soil and his plants that his garden seems to flourish most. Wildness, he has found, resides not only out there, but right here: in his soil, in his plants, even in himself…
But wildness is more a quality than a place, and though humans can't manufacture it, they can nourish and husband it…
The gardener cultivates wildness, but he does so carefully and respectfully, in full recognition of its mystery."

—Michael Pollan

Before you can finalize the list of seeds or cuttings that you will need to start your greenhouse garden, there is one other thing to consider: Which plants thrive in a greenhouse? Plenty of plants can grow in a greenhouse, from plants that provide aroma and aesthetics to plants that provide food for you and your loved ones.

It can be overwhelming to start researching plants and seeds and deciding which you would like to cultivate as a beginner. After all, there are about 391,000 species of plants in the world, and having to narrow this down to less than a hundred is a skill. One of the best ways to do this is to research the plants that thrive in a greenhouse before narrowing it down to which plants you like and share similar growing conditions to thrive within the same greenhouse. This process is called companion gardening.

In companion gardening, you place plants that benefit each other side by side. For example, placing a basil plant beside a tomato plant reduces your tomato plant's likelihood of hornworms. In general, companion gardening helps to deter pests in your greenhouse. Secondly, it helps decrease the number of pesticides and labor that your greenhouse will need to become pest-free. Thirdly, vegetable companion planting is well-known for increasing plant yields. Essentially, companion gardening dictates that you receive more plant yield for less gardening labor and materials.

VEGETABLES

Peppers (Bell & Chili)

Peppers are a very low-maintenance vegetable to plant. They need constant, moderate conditions that a greenhouse can easily provide, including a decent supply of sunlight, sufficient fertilizer, a regular water supply, and mulch covering. You may grow cayenne peppers, bell peppers, jalapeno peppers, and more. The spicier the pepper, the longer maturing period is required. To speed up this process, soak the seeds for ten minutes before planting. This soaking softens the seed cover, improving germination time.

Tomatoes

Tomato plants yield, on average, 2.75-5kg of tomatoes per plant. They grow and taste better when grown in full sun, so place your tomato plants on the side of the greenhouse that receives the most sunlight.

There are many breeds of tomatoes available for your greenhouse. With 25,000 varieties of tomatoes in the world, you should have no trouble finding a few for your greenhouse. Tomatoes grow best in rich, fertile soil with peat-free potting compost and plenty of shelter. You will need to water them regularly, and once they flower, your plants will need to be fed weekly, with a high potash fertilizer.

There are two main growing types: determinate (bush) and indeterminate (cordon). Bush growing types are generally planted in pots or hanging baskets, allowing their stems to trail around the edge. Cordon types are trained to grow tall, supported by a cane or stake. When growing cordon tomatoes, a stake is needed to support the plant. You will also need to pinch out any side shoots, as these prevent your plant from fruiting on one central stem.

Since you don't need to stake or pinch out bush tomato breeds, it may be wise to choose them for your first tomato plants.

Cucumbers

Greenhouse cucumbers need plenty of heat and don't need pollinating. You need to remove the male flowers to prevent pollination, failing which the fruits will taste bitter, growing full of seeds.

Carrots (& Other Roots)

Carrots are very easy to grow in a greenhouse. They are biennial, with many varieties being immune to diseases. Simply weed regularly and water at least an inch every week. Carrots like cool weather and can even tolerate frost. Carrots and other roots grow sweeter when grown in colder weather. You only need a small amount of general fertilizer once a week before sowing.

Turnips are cool-weather plants. Like carrots, they are also easy to grow, making them one of the best vegetables to grow in a greenhouse. They like plenty of sunlight, so place them in a position to receive constant sun. You will also need to ensure that the soil is well-drained and loosened to 12-15 inch depths.

Broccoli (& Cruciferous Vegetables)

Broccoli is another sun-loving and cool-season vegetable. Plant them in cold-frame greenhouses that support cold-season crops. They will need six to eight hours of total sun exposure each day.

Cabbages are the best vegetable to grow in a greenhouse. They are another cool-season vegetable that loves sunlight. Hence, do not let your greenhouse's temperature exceed 80°F, their best temperature. Cabbages very rapidly deplete the soil of resources. Don't plant them with other related species (other cruciferous vegetables). You should plant them close to beans and dill. Cabbages enrich the soil with nitrogen, while beans and dill attract wasps that destroy cabbage worms.

Squash

Keep the temperature in your greenhouse below 73 Fahrenheit for the perfect squash fruit. They are fast-growing if you use good quality soil. Do not water over the plants because this causes water to build up around the plant's neck, leading to rotting.

Peas

Another cool-season crop, peas grow best in winter greenhouses. The two most common pea varieties are snap and snow peas. Both varieties have the same growing requirements and thrive in both trailing and bush forms. Indeed, the plants thrive when grown in at least six hours of full sun each day and well-draining soil.

Peas love greenhouses because they offer a stable growing environment and help protect them from insects and pests.

Lettuce (& Other Leafy Greens)

Lettuce is a cold-season vegetable that can grow in frosty areas. In some frost-free areas, a greenhouse might even be unnecessary. Nonetheless, the extra protection and the stable environment of a greenhouse will bring you peace of mind during a cold spell. Lettuce loves cold weather so much that it will not grow in a greenhouse during the warm spring, summer, and fall months.

Lettuce is another plant that needs full sun exposure to grow. Place them in a sun-filled position within the greenhouse because they need to receive at least six hours of direct sun daily. You must fill the bed with loamy topsoil and root care leaving two inches of space at the top for compost. Then, using a garden fork, mix the compost thoroughly with the topsoil down six to eight inches. The best fertilizer for lettuce is balanced fertilizer—such as a 10-10-10 formula blended into the soil.

FRUITS

Did You Know?

The first-ever documented case of a carrot was 5,000 years ago when they were used for medicine.

Lemons

Lemons grow best in a temperature-controlled greenhouse at between 70 and 90 degrees Fahrenheit. Lemons, like carrots, are another simple plant to grow because they require very little care. Nonetheless, lemon trees grown inside greenhouses may sometimes develop pest infestations, so monitor your tree very carefully to ensure it stays healthy.

It might be best to plant dwarf lemon tree varieties, such as Dwarf Lisbon. This choice considers the size of your greenhouse since this variety is much smaller than a standard lemon tree yet bears similarly large, palatable fruit. Place the lemon tree close to the southern side of the greenhouse. Here, it will receive at least six to eight hours of sunlight daily. To prevent leaf scald, position the tree one to two feet away from the glass.

Regular, moderate watering is a necessity for your lemon plant. Water your lemon tree whenever the top three inches of soil feel dry. Water regularly until the soil feels moderately moist in the top five inches.

Apricots

Apricots are very delicate plants to nurture. They flower very early (the first of all the fruit trees to open their blossoms) in late February and early March. Since the weather is far too unpredictable to offer reliable pollination, this often causes poor fruit yield, inadequate pollination, and frost damage to the flowers.

Place your apricot plant in the sunniest side of the greenhouse—the south or west wall—but make sure that it is also sheltered. Be aware that apricots are so delicate that they sometimes die for no discernible reason. To mitigate this, ensure that you give them the best of care.

They like well-drained, well-cultivated soil that is not too dry, and they love a little fertilizer after you plant them.

Oranges

One of the best reasons for cultivating orange and other citrus trees is the beautiful aroma they release into your greenhouse. Organic, lovingly-grown oranges and lemons, when harvested, can leave your kitchen smelling divine too.

Small citrus trees grow very well in northern greenhouses, but you will need to keep your greenhouse warm in the winter since citrus trees do not grow naturally in cold climates. Keep the temperature at a minimum of 50 degrees Fahrenheit. This allows you to balance the cost of heating your greenhouse daily with providing enough warmth to keep your orange tree alive (preventing it from dropping its leaves). Growth will slow down at 50 degrees Fahrenheit but will continue sufficiently to keep your citrus tree alive.

In spring and summer, you will need to water and fertilize your tree daily, but minimally in the colder months. With proper care, expect a bountiful harvest from your tree in the summer.

Grapes

Grapes grown in a greenhouse are usually sweeter and of better quality. Grapevines tend to take up a lot of room; if you have a small greenhouse, plant just one vine and grow it in a tub. The two main varieties used are Black Hamburg, which produces large black grapes, and Thomspon's Seedless, which produces green grapes.

If you have a larger greenhouse, plant your grapevine with the root outside, but you must be willing to make a hole through your greenhouse. Grapevines have extensive root systems. For this reason, it is advised to plant them with their roots outside. By doing so, you allow the root to expand and seek the moisture and nutrients it needs, meaning that you may not have to water it yourself as often. If you have a small or medium-sized greenhouse, this method may be preferable too since it allows you to free up space inside.

If you plant the roots inside, your tree benefits from warmer soil, contributing to earlier growth; however, this does bring disadvantages of requiring irrigation and greater attention and care from you.

Strawberries

Your greenhouse will protect your strawberries from heavy rain and strong winds and provide enough heat to encourage out-of-season fruit-bearing. Strawberries enjoy a lot of heat, light, and dry conditions. They need to be exposed to at least six hours of sunlight per day with a daily temperature of about 60 degrees Fahrenheit.

They have shallow roots that dry out quickly, so they will need constant watering. During the growing season, they need to be fed with fertilizer once every two weeks.

Apples

Apples are native to cold winter regions and thrive at lower temperatures. Apple trees have fewer issues if grown outdoors; indoors, you must watch out for drought and heat stress. Since they cannot grow without considerably cold weather, you will have to plant them with other cold-season plants, like carrots.

Apples need vernalization (at least 900 to 1,200 hours of temperatures below 45 degrees Fahrenheit every year). Apple trees also need sufficient sunlight and well-drained, moist and fertile soil. Furthermore, they will need to be pollinated if you want them to produce fruit.

Olive Trees

To grow olive trees in greenhouses, you will need to choose an olive plant variety that can grow in containers, like the Arbequina Olive tree. Plant other varieties of olive trees, like the Leccino olive tree, near your Arbequina Olive tree if you want it to produce more olives. The Leccino olive tree can also survive colder weather and grows well in regions where the winter temperature reaches 50 degrees—just above freezing.

Do not plant olive trees in soil that does not drain well as their roots hate being damp or wet. Notwithstanding, younger olive trees can thrive if you keep them slightly more moist than mature trees.

ORNAMENTAL PLANTS

Did You Know?

Bay leaves are toxic for bugs and pests. Like garlic, ginger, and turmeric, bay leaves were traditionally used as insect and pest repellents. They are a non-toxic option for humans compared to chemical-based repellents.

Geraniums

Geraniums are easy to grow. When grown in a greenhouse, geraniums will need plenty of light with six to eight hours of sunlight and temperatures of 65 - 70 degrees Fahrenheit during the day and 55 degrees Fahrenheit at night. Use moist, well-draining potting soil with equal amounts of soil, peat, and perlite.

Use a simple water-soluble houseplant fertilizer with additional organic matter every four to six weeks throughout your plant's active growing season.

Impatiens

Impatiens are annuals that can be propagated very easily from seeds or cuttings. They are highly water-sensitive and will wilt quickly if thirsty. They enjoy moist, well-draining soil. Keep them in partial or deep shade away from full sun and fertilize them every two weeks using water-soluble fertilizer.

Petunias

There are four varieties of petunias. They all love regular watering and plenty of sunlight. They can grow when partially shaded, but you can promote frequent and multiple blooms in full sunlight.

Fertilize them weekly with balanced, water-soluble fertilizer designed for blooming plants.

Salvias

Salvias are low-maintenance plants that need average soil to thrive. A relative of the mint plant, they also enjoy partly shaded to sunny environments. When salvia is in bloom, its sweet smell attracts plenty of butterflies and other pollinators. They are rapid growers that can tolerate heat well.

It is best to let the roots of salvias dry out before rewatering. Nevertheless, different varieties of salvia prefer different growing conditions; for example, the Japanese yellow sage likes rich, moist soil and shade.

Caladiums

You must plant Caladiums at the right time. The right time varies depending on where you live, based on USDA planting zones. Check out your zone at https://planthardiness.ars.usda.gov/PHZMWeb/. The right time to plant is:

- Hardiness zones 9, 10: March 15
- Hardiness zone 8: April 15
- Hardiness zone 7: May 1
- Hardiness zone 6: June 1
- Hardiness zones 3, 4, 5: June 15

Caladiums love well-drained soil and shade. They can tolerate six to eight hours of full sunlight, during which they require more water than usual. They show deeper color when grown in the sun than in the shade.

Ferns

These are easy to grow as long as you keep them away from drafts, dry air, and temperature extremes. Some varieties love hot weather and full sun, and others prefer cooler temperatures and shade. Your fern variety of fern will dictate the perfect conditions.

Per contra, all ferns love humid environments. Mist your ferns at regular intervals with tepid, soft water unless the humidity of your greenhouse is already very high. Ferns are forest and woodland plants with tender, delicate roots that love compost, rich in leaf mold and decayed vegetable matter. Most varieties prefer morning or late afternoon sun or regular dim light with periodic breaks of bright sunlight. They do not like cold but thrive at different heat levels, so check your variety carefully for its ideal temperature.

Poinsettias

Poinsettias are high-maintenance plants, needing proper water, light, and temperature conditions. While in full bloom, poinsettias love semi-cool, humid conditions and bright but indirect light. They also crave plenty of moisture, but you must ensure adequate drainage because they like plenty of water and can also easily drown. If you plan to keep your poinsettia plant after bloom, move it to a cool, dark area until spring or around April.

Chrysanthemums

Chrysanthemums need extra care, so choose the right chrysanthemum flower based on your region. If you are in a northern area, plant hardy chrysanthemums in spring because they are more likely to survive. In southern areas, plant mums in spring or autumn. Fall gives your mums the most significant benefit because they can avoid the summer heat.

Use well-draining, organic soil and sun-lit positions.

Pansies

Pansies bloom in colder climates. Hybrid varieties can withstand heat more than those of the past with more prominent blooms. Pansies are biennials meaning that they may not grow until the second year after they are planted. They will thrive if you prepare the soil very well, adding compost and organic material, like rotten leaves, to your soil before planting pansies—these plants like well-draining soil and lots of nutrients.

Coleus

Also known as painted nettle or poor man's croton, coleus comes in various leaf sizes and plant shapes. You can place them in any area of your greenhouse.

Coleus propagates and roots very easily. Cuttings can be propagated in a simple glass of water. They thrive in fertile, well-draining soil and partial shade, proliferating under these conditions. Many varieties can tolerate the sun, however.

Keep them well-watered and use half-strength liquid fertilizer once in a while in spring and summer.

Gazania

Gazanias are very easy to grow, even in hot weather, but they do not like poor, dry, or sandy soil. They are simple to grow because all they need is to be watered. While drought resistant, they bloom bigger when watered regularly.

- There are plenty of plants that you can grow in a greenhouse.
- When choosing plants, research the plants that thrive in a greenhouse before narrowing your search to those YOU like.